SWERVE

Life Altering Wisdom

from Saints, Masters,

and

People Like You and Me

KEVIN CULLEN

A POST HILL PRESS BOOK
ISBN: 978-1-63758-034-9
ISBN (eBook): 978-1-63758-035-6

Swerve:
Life Altering Wisdom from Saints, Masters, and People Like You and Me
© 2021 by Kevin Cullen
All Rights Reserved

Post Hill Press
New York • Nashville
posthillpress.com

Published in the United States of America
1 2 3 4 5 6 7 8 9 10

This book is dedicated to all of the special people in my life who have taught me, inspired me, shared life with me, laughed with me and loved me. I would like to make a special mention of one person in particular—my mother, Nuala Cullen. She is one of the greatest people I have ever known; anyone that knows her will attest. There is no one like her and there will never be. At ninety-four years old, she is still going strong; she is the epitome of love, compassion, common sense, integrity and grit all rolled into one. I am very privileged to call her my mother, and I have the extraordinary life that I do largely because of her. I love you, Mom!

ACKNOWLEDGMENTS

A s any author will tell you, writing a book is a holistic process, and the content comes from somewhere other than what's in one's brain. In many ways, they will tell you that a book organically unfolds in a way that it feels like "it is writing itself" sometimes as one goes through living their life. On the other hand, I will attest that writing well is not as easy as it may seem and a lot of hard work goes into it. There are people behind the scenes who have contributed greatly to the writing of *SWERVE* and without their unique contribution, this book would not be possible.

My rock—Let me start with Janeice Weinand, my wife (going on twenty years) and very best friend. She is one of the finest people I have ever known; saintly in too many ways to list. Those who know Janeice know exactly what I mean.

Amazing clients—With our consulting practice at Leadera, I have some very special clients, some of whom have been working with me for over twenty years. They have allowed me to contribute to them both personally and professionally and in turn, I have learned a ton from them about leadership, integrity, character, and grit. They are Elizabeth Killinger, Ian Fillinger, Randa Duncan, Mike Putzke, and Karen Taylor. Each of these people are uniquely extraordinary leaders in their own right and I have had the unique privilege to work for them during my career.

My first boss—Jimmy Murphy—was one of the founders of Brendan Vacations. I started there working for him in the mailroom, sending out travel brochures to travel agents. Jimmy was born to be in the travel business; it was his divine calling and he was both passionate and superb at it. He was also an amazing businessman. He taught me how to do business the right way, to run a company with integrity and to respect, appreciate, and honor his employees. I learned most everything I needed to know about business from Jimmy at a very young age.

Coaches—I have had some excellent coaches, teachers, and mentors during my professional career and each of them have played a significant role in *SWERVE*. Elizabeth Harper Neeld is an author of more than twenty-five books. Elizabeth spent several years as my writing coach. She taught me the discipline of writing, she trained me to think like a writer, and above all, she taught me how to be a writer. Debby Englander coached me in the art and science of publishing a book. Debby is a gem of a human being; a New Yorker through and through who has spent her career in the publishing business and knows her stuff. Debby is tough as nails on the outside and believe me, sometimes she had to be, but with a soft cream center on the inside and a wonderful sense of humor. I absolutely love working with Debby. Sarah Cook Flatow is the best executive coach I have ever encountered. Her work is transformational and profound. Sarah worked as my coach for several years and her work with me changed the course of my life to working with a greater purpose.

The name for *SWERVE*—Su Mathews Hale is a renowned branding expert who spent the first part of her career working as a partner for one of the top "Madison Avenue" design firms. A while back, she transitioned from her Madison Avenue career and founded her own firm, Su Mathews Hale Design, which is thriving because of her reputation and talent. Su and her team have helped our consulting firm with our brand, our message, and graphics; they really do phenomenal work. I asked them to help me with the name the book. After interviewing me, they made three suggestions—*SWERVE* immediately jumped of the page at me. Everyone that saw it loved it, including the publisher. Thank you to the SMHD team for your creativity and genius.

Administration—I have had some wonderful colleagues who have worked with me administratively as part of my team. Many of the words in this book they pored over through countless versions and re-writes. These people are my unsung heroes and have been a blessing to partner with. They are Karla Ziegler, Sara Carpenter, Margie Frank, Amanda Chaney, Alex Cook, and Katy Belcher. Gina Donato helped with copyrighted material and worked tirelessly throughout the entire publishing process.

Special recognition—to Landmark Worldwide where I worked for sixteen years. There I had the honor of working side by side with the founder Werner Erhard and had the privilege of leading the Landmark Forum for tens of thousands of people. In working at Landmark, I learned so much about myself, about people, and about life and how to make the world a better place to live in. If you've never done that program, I highly recommend it.

Special friends—I have some incredible friends who have been there for me at my greatest and toughest moments. They have empowered me to be my best and not settle for less. They are Brooks Hale, Michaela Curran, Nancy Skallerup, and Tom Phelan.

Encouragement to write this book—A few people gave me special support in the writing of SWERVE: Betty Stoub, Shirley Rouse, Sue Watson, and Heather King.

Saints and Masters—In closing, I would like to appreciate just a few of the incredible Saints and Masters that were the inspiration for SWERVE: Mother Teresa, His Holiness the Dalai Lama, Werner Erhard , Dr. Choe, Papaji, H.W.L. Poonja , Gangaji, and Lynne Twist. It is mastery that allows humanity to elevate and fulfill our destiny.

TABLE OF CONTENTS

INTRODUCTION

"If you do not change direction, you may end up where you are heading."

– Old Chinese proverb

We are all creatures of habit. You probably drink the same coffee at about the same time every morning. You take the same route to work every day or park in the same spot.

We prefer a familiar and predictable routine. However, doing the same thing the same way won't lead to change. If you are a leader who wants vastly different results, from more engaged employees to higher profits and satisfied clients, then you have to disrupt things. If you want to make a real change, you need to stop doing just what's comfortable. I'm not talking about making changes just for the sake of change—I am talking about the kind of change that creates a new possibility for the future.

I have spent forty years working in the field of transformation and have worked with well over a quarter of a million people. I've worked side by side with globally recognized pioneers and experts in both personal and organizational transformation. I have consulted and coached CEOs, executives, managers, and front-line workers at leading organizations. One of my most profound and simple discoveries is this: organizations are perfectly designed to produce the results they deliver—nothing more and nothing less. Without some major disruption, an organization or person will almost certainly continue to do what they have always done because that is what they are designed to do.

Many professionals would consider that success. In sailing, we refer to this as "hold your course and speed," which is the ultimate goal—keeping it steady. However, that kind of complacency will not produce breakthroughs in your business or in your life. It will not deliver extraordinary results; it will deliver *more of the same*.

If you are interested in achieving almost unimaginable results, you have to understand that *breakthroughs require disruption*. To be an effective disruptor, you must be bold, be willing to take risks, and have an extraordinary level of integrity. Thus, the name of the book, *SWERVE,* which implies changing direction quickly to avoid a collision ahead—the almost certain future.

Being a creature of habit does not lend itself to change. I have spent my career working with people who want to make changes and I can tell you one thing about us—we *resist* change. This book is about the ability to change your course in life and in business, with small matters and large ones. It is about learning how to pay attention to life in such a way that you recognize the need to shift and are able to do so when the situation calls for it.

This book will take you on a journey of *disruption* that lays out the steps and highlights the qualities you will need to be an effective disruptor both. You will learn valuable lessons that will involve changing the way you think, speak, and act. In turn, it will allow you to inspire the people around you to also transform.

While *SWERVE* offers advice for business leaders based largely on my work over the last two decades, I also know how disruption can affect one as an individual. Here, I'll share how I met Mother Teresa—she changed everything I thought about charity that had been drilled into me during my twelve years attending Catholic school. That one conversation with her had a profound impact on me; it disrupted how I think, speak, and act. It changed my behavior forever. *SWERVE* is about changing the way you operate, in your professional and personal life.

In this book, I will show you how:

o   To learn to recognize situations that require a shift in perspective or change in behavior

o   To overcome your fear of change and not let anything stop you

o   To efficiently make changes quickly and easily

o   To change the way you communicate with employees, clients, customers, friends, and family

o   To be a change agent for transforming the culture of your company

o   To discover the wisdom that lives all around you

CHAPTER 1

THE GREATEST GIFT IN LIFE

One of the greatest honors of my life was meeting His Holiness, the Dalai Lama, and spending some time with him discussing topics that pertained to humanity and the state of the world. This came about because I was teaching a course in Salt Lake City for about one hundred people. One of the participants was a Tibetan lady by the name of Khando Chazotsang, who, it turns out, was a relative of His Holiness. When the course was ending, Khando came up to meet me and asked if I would consider delivering a seminar for the staff who worked directly for His Holiness in India.

Quite honestly, I was a bit surprised by this invitation. I smiled and said I was very honored but surely a group of Buddhists would not find "enlightenment" from the kind of things we covered in the seminar she had just participated in. She lightly disagreed and described the staff's stressful situation and conditions, which had to do with constant pressure and threats from China. She went on to say that the life skills she had gained from the seminar would greatly help the group navigate their stressful conditions and the relief I offered would allow them to serve His Holiness at a whole new level. I told her that I had no current plans to be in India in the near future, but I would keep it in mind if I had the chance to travel to India. She thanked me and said goodnight.

I couldn't stop thinking about her requests. It seemed like an honor and a unique opportunity to experience something special and make a difference. Her invitation stayed on my mind; I kept coming back to it no matter what I did. Soon after, I left my job and decided to take a sabbatical, which would involve study, spiritual work and reflection, and travel. I decided to go to somewhere I had never been. I thought about many places, but I kept coming back to the invitation from Khando, and it just made sense to go to India. It was somewhere I had never been and had always wanted to visit and experience. The spiritual aspect was also a plus.

I contacted Khando in late October and let her know I was available to deliver the training for the course she described back in Salt Lake City. She was delighted and asked me to give her time to plan.

Shortly thereafter, she contacted me and said that His Holiness' staff was extremely busy and that they would not be able to participate during the month that I was planning to visit. However, she had arranged a private meeting for me with His Holiness! I would hear from his office as to when the meeting would take place.

It was Christmas Eve, 1995. My parents were visiting, and we were sitting in the living room when the mail slot flipped open with incoming mail. There were a few Christmas cards, some bills, and an unusual envelope made of the crinkly, lightweight paper that was typical back then for airmail letters. It was from Dharamsala, India, and it was from the office of His Holiness, the Dalai Lama.

I held the envelope in my hand and stared at it for a few moments, contemplating what it might contain. My mother noticed my fascination with the letter and asked me what it was. I said that it looked like a letter from the Dalai Lama, and I opened it carefully, not tearing the envelope. The letter was short and to point:

> You are scheduled to meet with His Holiness the Dalai Lama on April 24, 1995, at 2 PM at his home in Dharamsala, India.
>
> – Tenzin Dhonden, Secretary for His Holiness, the Dalai Lama

"What does it say?" asked my mom.

I said, "I have a meeting with the Dalai Lama in India in April."

"Are you going to go?" she asked.

I looked up and said, "Of course I am—no question!"

Her next comment was both surprising and funny. "You know he is not Catholic," she said with a concerned smile.

"Yes mom, I have heard he is not Catholic—this is like being invited to meet the Buddha reincarnated. I wouldn't miss this for the world. This is a great privilege."

Christmas Eve happens to be my birthday; needless to say, it was an amazing birthday present. I was humbled, honored, and excited all at once. I kept thinking about it, imagining what it would be like to travel to India and meet His Holiness.

A bit of background on the Dalai Lama:

The Dalai Lama was born Lhamo Thondup on July 6, 1935 in Taktser, China to a peasant family. In 1937, the child was declared the reincarnation of a great Buddhist spiritual leader and re-named Tenzin Gyatso, the future leader of Tibetan Buddhism as the fourteenth Dalai Lama. At age fifteen, he assumed political power of Tibet as the Dalai Lama. The People's Republic of China invaded that same year. Fearing assassination, he and thousands of followers fled to Dharamsala in northern India, where they established an alternative government. Since then, the Dalai Lama has taken numerous actions in hopes of establishing an autonomous Tibetan state within the People's Republic of China. However, the Chinese government has shown no signs of moving toward peace and reconciliation with Tibet. The Dalai Lama has also conducted hundreds of conferences, lectures, and workshops worldwide, as part of his humanitarian efforts. He was awarded the Nobel Peace Prize in 1989. In December 2008, the Dalai Lama announced his semi-retirement after having gallstone surgery.[1]

Dalai Lamas are believed to be the reincarnation of Avalokiteshvara, an important Buddhist deity and

---

[1] Wikipedia contributors. 2021. "14th Dalai Lama." Wikipedia, The Free Encyclopedia. June 26, 2021. https://en.wikipedia.org/w/index.php?title=14th_Dalai_Lama&oldid=1030523663.

the personification of compassion. Dalai Lamas are also enlightened beings who have postponed their own afterlife and chosen to take rebirth to benefit humanity. "Dalai" means "ocean" in Mongolian (the name "Gyatso" comes from the Tibetan word for ocean).

Lama" is the equivalent of the Sanskrit word "guru" or spiritual teacher. Put together, the title of Dalai Lama is literally "Ocean Teacher," meaning a "teacher spiritually as deep as the ocean."

Here is a little information regarding Buddhism:

Buddhism was created in the sixth century BCE with the birth of Buddha Siddhartha Gautama, making it one of the oldest religions practiced today. Originating in India, the religion spread throughout most of eastern and southern Asia. Buddhism came to Tibet in the eighth century CE. Unlike other religions that are centered on a supreme being, Buddhism is centered on four basic truths: life is not perfect; people are left unsatisfied by trying to make life perfect; people can realize there is a better way to achieve fulfillment; and by living one's life through wisdom, ethical conduct, and mental discipline, people will reach enlightenment.[2]

As I planned my trip to India, I shared my excitement with several friends, and some asked if they could come along on the

---

2   Ibid.

adventure. Of course, I said yes to everyone who asked, and the group grew. As its size expanded, so did the itinerary. I decided also to visit Calcutta and do some volunteer work in Mother Teresa's Kalighat Home for the Sick and Dying Destitutes. I added a trip to Lucknow to visit a guru named Papaji and, of course, I wanted to visit the Taj Mahal in Agra, along with the ancient spiritual capital of India, Varanasi.

Before long, there were fourteen of us heading on this adventure that we later referred to as "The Magical Mystery Tour." After we travelled through Nepal and across India from Calcutta, having seen and experienced some truly remarkable things, we arrived in New Delhi for a few days and prepared for our long bus trip up to Dharamsala, which lies in the North, close to the Himalayas.

We boarded a rickety bus and headed on our "twelve-hour journey" with two native drivers who spoke no English and didn't give the impression that they knew what they were doing. It was a long haul, and when the sun started to go down, I went to the back of the bus and laid across the seats for a nice, long nap.

Hours later, I was awakened by my friend Michaela's screams of terror, "We're all going to die!" I got up, headed to the front of the bus and signaled for the driver to stop. I asked my friends what all the commotion was about, and I got them to speak slowly one at a time. Someone told me we were lost and somewhere in Pakistan, someone else told me we had almost driven off several cliffs, and yet another friend said that these drivers had no idea where they were or where were going.

I asked the driver to open the door so I could take a leak. As I stood there, taking care of business in the faint light of the bus headlights, I saw a small sign that said "Dharamsala: 2 km." I then escorted the three hysterical passengers out to the sign and told them it was a four-minute walk to our destination. Everyone calmed down, and we headed to the small town that His Holiness calls home. It was late and we were tired, but we found the inn where we would be staying. The hotel attendant told me that Richard Gere had stayed in the same room I was assigned just before we arrived. I probably should have been impressed, but I was too exhausted and just wanted to go to sleep; our twelve-hour bus ride had taken twenty long, eventful hours.

The next morning, we were up early to explore the village of Dharamsala, which has become home for the exiled Tibetan community. It was different than all of the other places we had been in India. Situated in the Himalayan mountains, as the home of His Holiness, its air was filled with a quiet, peaceful joy that was palpable. There was a sense of stillness that was quite calming and healing, and there was almost a meditative state that permeated the entire village. The people we passed along the street and in the shops flashed infectious smiles. Wherever we went, we became aware of the richness and devotion of the Tibetans who thrive in their home away from their home.

Our appointment was later that afternoon. We were all excited and a bit nervous, knowing that we were going to meet and speak with someone who was so widely known, respected, and adored throughout the world. We were asked to arrive an hour early so we could be checked in. This involved being interviewed, processed, and strip-searched by members of the Indian army who were fully equipped with machine guns. It was such an ironic juxtaposition that we were meeting with one of the most peace-loving human beings on the planet, yet we had to pass through weaponry and careful scrutiny to be in his presence. We were directed down a path to the residence and told that His Holiness had been engaged in silent meditation for six weeks prior to our visit. That made me curious about what kind of mood he would be in. In what seemed to be a large living room containing altars, tapestries, a throne, and thankas that hung around the room, we were seated around a small table where two chairs were left empty.

His Holiness came in with an exuberant smile, open arms, and in a very pleasant deep voice he proclaimed, "Welcome to Dharamsala—our temporary home since 1955," letting out an enthusiastic laugh. He sat with us and asked us to introduce ourselves, asked us questions about where we were from, and took some time to get to know us a bit. He was genuinely curious about where we had been and what we had seen. He wanted to know what we thought of India and gave us room to share whatever we cared to.

He listened intensely and earnestly. Then the conversation shifted a bit when he shared the journey of the Tibetan people and their culture with us. When he spoke about the Chinese government, he was notably respectful and reverent, which I didn't expect. He was living in exile from his native home with his culture under constant threat, and he spoke with kindness and sensitivity about the very people who caused it.

It was obvious that we were sitting in front of someone who saw the world more differently than anyone I had ever met. He gave us a chance to ask him anything. We had come with lots of questions to ask, but when given the opportunity, we were fairly quiet—his presence had answered many of our questions in a nonverbal way. Nevertheless, we managed to ask a few questions in no apparent order. We discussed the Buddhist traditions, which led to a conversation about abortion and the importance of silence.

It was getting to the end of our time with His Holiness when my dear friend, Brooks, asked him a truly profound question: "What is the greatest gift in life?" It was an amazing question and the perfect one to ask this wise master. (I wished that I had thought of it, but good for you, Brooks.) His Holiness looked us and stopped. He scratched his head for a second and said, "That is a very good question, let me think for a moment." I thought, *Doesn't he already know the answer to that question? I would think that the reincarnation of Buddha would have that at his fingertips.*

When he finally spoke, he said, "Yes. I know the answer to your question—the greatest gift in life is compassion. Yes, that's it. Compassion is the greatest gift in life." The room became still for a moment as we took in what he had said. We thanked him for his time and the honor of meeting him. As part of a traditional ceremony when in his presence, he bestowed each of us with a silk scarf called a *khata*. Consistent with the tradition, we each bowed as he placed it over our heads and around our necks, and we left in a quiet, meditative silence that filled each of us with a sacred kind of energy.

No one will ever forget or not be touched by what happened in that room. I immediately began to pay attention to compassion. I tried to practice it in everything I did. Whenever I was in somebody's presence, I would try to get into their mindset to understand that if I had their life circumstances, I would probably think, speak, and act much in the same way they did. With people who were in more unfortunate circumstances, I tried to embrace the philosophy of "there but for the grace of God go I" but always with compassion. Sometimes I did it well, sometimes I didn't.

I practiced compassion for over a year, and then one day it dawned on me that I had made a mistake. I noticed that I was being extremely hard on myself about whatever I'd done that I didn't like. It became clear that I had been practicing compassion for everyone around me, but I had none for myself. In other words, I could accept everyone else's behaviors, faults, and mistakes, but when it came to my own, I had no tolerance and no ability to accept my flaws. I thought, *If I don't have compassion for myself and don't practice it with myself, I neither have the ability nor business showing it to others because it's not real compassion.*

Compassion is about allowing, including, and accepting things and people as they are and life as it exists. What a profound insight to discover the gift of compassion—the greatest gift in life. Live it in such a way that you embrace life on its own terms. Albert Einstein once said:

> A human being is a part of the whole, called by us "Universe," a part limited in time and space. He experiences himself, his thoughts and feelings as something separated from the rest—a kind of optical delusion of his consciousness. This delusion is a kind of prison for us, restricting us to our personal desires and to affection for a few persons nearest to us. Our task must be to free ourselves from this prison by widening our circle of compassion

to embrace all living creatures and the whole of nature in its beauty.[3]

He called our living without compassion a "prison" that we must free ourselves from. These are two of the greatest thinkers in history, so it's well worth taking their advice and live with compassion.

3 Popova, Maria. n.d. "Einstein on Widening Our Circles of Compassion." BrainPickings.Org. Accessed June 27, 2021. https://www.brainpickings. org/2016/11/28/einstein-circles-of-compassion/.

CHAPTER 2

START
WITH INTEGRITY

I cannot say enough about the importance of having and operating with integrity and living consistently with your values and principles.

To be clear, everyone already knows this intellectually. But there is a distinction between knowing something and acting on something. It took me most of my life to learn this. Now, mind you, I was taught from a young age what was right and what was wrong. I knew I should do the right thing but that didn't mean I lived that way. In fact, I would say that much of my life was spent figuring out ways around this idea and trying to get away with what I could.

When I say that, I am not talking about being a thief, gangster, or anything like that. Instead, I had a habit of telling white lies or cheating where I though no one would notice, and it probably wouldn't matter. Then I would rationalize it or justify what I had done; it seemed so insignificant that I thought I had gotten away with it. Let me say this—you NEVER get away with it. The universe knows and so do you, and you will unconsciously settle the score. I am not kidding about this—it happens every time and just because you don't notice it that doesn't mean it doesn't happen; it may be that you are unconscious.

I certainly was for a great part of my life. Having a lack of integrity makes you numb, sometimes so much that you are oblivious to what is happening and how your actions play out in the big picture of your life.

Even though I knew integrity was important, I only knew it intellectually but did not have a real appreciation for how it works in the world. My epiphany took place when I did some intense coaching with a woman named Sarah Cook-Flatow. When I say intense, I mean two all-day sessions every six to eight weeks for several years. Part of the coaching required that I agree to three promises that would require me to operate in line with my values, principles, and ideals, so it seemed easy and straightforward. All I had to do was live my life in a way that didn't cause difficulties for myself or others. She would start each session by asking me if I had kept the last agreements we had made regarding problems, upsets, and withholds. If I had violations with any of the three, we would not start the session—instead, we would work on integrity. At first, it was like getting caught; I felt stupid, foolish, ashamed, and embarrassed. Here I was, a full grown adult, and I didn't seem to be able to keep three simple promises.

After a while, I found myself avoiding the drama of having to cop to it by simply keeping the agreements. As a result, I began noticing that things went more my way. It felt magical—lights turned green, doors opened, and amazing things began to happen. It was like I was having great luck, but it wasn't luck, it was my having integrity for the first time.

One of the things that I learned is that it is normal to have good fortune, serendipitous blessings, and miracles. They happen naturally; however, these things shrivel up and disappear when your integrity is absent. I cannot prove this, but I could introduce you to a thousand people who would corroborate that statement. More importantly, anyone who lives their life with true integrity KNOWS this. Miracles are normal and natural—if they don't occur in your life, check your integrity.

There is an article we use in one of our courses called "Integrity: Without It Nothing Works" by Karen Christiansen. It is an interview with Michael Jensen, a professor emeritus from Harvard Business School. Jensen is a well-known economist who has dedicated the past decade to empowering people to be extraordinary leaders. In the interview, Jensen makes the case for integrity in business:

> Integrity is a necessary condition for maximum performance. That is, if something is in integrity – is whole, complete, unbroken – it has maximum workability. But because it takes more than workability (a product of integrity) alone to realize maximum performance, integrity is not a sufficient condition for maximum performance.[4]

---

4   Jensen, Michael C., "Integrity: Without it Nothing Works" (April 6, 2014). Rotman Magazine: The Magazine of the Rotman School of Management, pp. 16-20, Fall 2009, Harvard Business School NOM Unit Working Paper No. 10-042, Barbados Group Working Paper No. 09-04, Simon School Working Paper No. FR 10-01, Available at SSRN: https://ssrn.com/abstract=1511274.

He goes on to define to say that integrity is *honoring ones' word*. A person's word consists of the following:

1. *What you said* you will do or will not do, and if you do it, doing it on time.

2. *What you know* to do or not do, and if you do it, doing it the way it is meant to be done on time, unless you have explicitly said otherwise.

3. *What is expected* of you to do or not do (even when not explicitly expressed), and if you do it, doing it on time, unless you have explicitly otherwise.

4. *What you say is so* whenever you have given your word as to the existence of some thing or some state. Your word includes being willing to be held accountable for evidence of what you have asserted.

5. *What you say you stand for* whether expressed in the form of a declaration made to one or more people, or even to yourself, as well as what you hold yourself out to others as standing for. (This can formally declared or not.)

6. *Social and moral standards* expressed in group ethical standards and governmental legal standards of right and wrong, and good and bad behavior in society, in which one enjoys the benefits of membership are also part of one's word unless a) one has explicitly and publicly expressed an intention to not keep one or more of these standards, and b) one is willing to bear the costs of refusing to conform to these standards.

When I became aware of what integrity consisted of at this level, it was eye-opening. Examining it deeply cleared up all the mysteries and confusion. I had never understood it at the level of what we do on a day-to-day basis—for me, integrity was always more like a theme or a concept. My newfound awareness of it opened up a whole new level of possibility for me and workability showed up like I never thought it would. Consistent with what Jensen said: "Performance-improved results, [and] amazing results became the norm."

Someone once shared with me a piece from the Maliwada Training School, and I invite you to read it. It's an amazing way to look at integrity.

ON INTEGRITY

Maliwada Human Development Training School

We are going to visit the arena of Profound Humanness called "Integrity". Sometimes "integrity" is reduced to mean a kind of moral uprightness and steadfastness, in the sense of saying, "He has too much integrity to ever take a bribe."

But profound integrity goes far beyond this. Sometimes, in order to distinguish it from more limited popular usage, it is called "secondary integrity". This is the integrity, which is not constrained by limited moralities, however well-intentioned. The integrity that is profound living is the singularity of thrust of a life committed and ordering every dimension of the self towards that commitment. Thus the self is in fact shaped by the self, and focused towards that commitment. You can say that an audacious creation of the self takes place in integrity, without which you are simply the creation of the various forces impacting you in your society.

Thus the basis of integrity is a destinal resolve - a resolve that chooses and sets your destiny and out of which your whole life is ordered. The object of that resolve is the ultimate decision of each person, and each person makes that choice, consciously or unconsciously. To do so with awareness is the height of man's responsibility. It is incarnate freedom. It is what real freedom looks like.

When man has thus exercised his freedom he realizes that to be true to himself ever thereafter he has a unique position to look at the values of his society. He is no longer bound by the opinions and codes of his fellow-man, but reevaluates then on the basis of their impact on his destinal resolve.

Thus, the man of integrity is continuously engaged in a societal transvaluation, a moving across the values of society and reinterpreting them in line with his life's thrust. It does not give him the liberty of ignoring his society, but his obligation transcends the conformity of living within the codes and mores of his society. Thus the man of profound integrity always seems to not quite fit with his fellow-men, but his actions always are appropriate for him, even to those who oppose him.

No matter how odd the man of profound integrity appears to his neighbors, he experiences himself as securely anchored. While he is very clear that this world is not his home, nevertheless he experiences himself as having found his native vale. He experiences an eternal at-one-ness, not so much with the currents and waves of activity around him, but with the deeper trends of history itself. Amid the flux of wavering to and fro that is so evident in others, he experiences an inexplicable rootedness, as though he has sunk a taproot deep into the foundations of the earth itself. Though he experiences his life as a long journey, even an endless journey, towards the object of his resolve, yet he never senses himself as a stranger on the journey It's as if he'd been there before. Original integrity is experienced primarily by this sense of at-one-ness.

Kierkegaard once write a book about this kind of integrity that he titled, "Purity of Heart is to Will One Thing". An ancient philosopher focused his wisdom around this integrity with the advice, "Know yourself, and to your own self, be true."

This document comes from the curriculum of the Maliwada Human Development Training School in Maliwada, India, which is a former program of ICA International. They are not certain of the year, so there are no further details that they could provide for a citation.

I believe these words are spoken by Joseph Wesley Mathews, the founder of the Institute of Cultural Affairs, who laid out a vision of 24 Human Development Projects.[5]

In conclusion, it is actually pretty simple. Live consistent with your ideals, values, and principles, and when you violate them, clean them up. When you operate this way, you maximize possibility of performance, satisfaction, and fulfillment. It's not easy; in fact, it takes a lot of work. But it's worth it, I promise.

The ideas in this chapter were originated by Werner Erhard and developed further with his co-authors Professor Michael Jensen and Steve Zaffron and are used with permission.

---

5   "On Integrity." n.d. Gathering Village. Accessed June 27, 2021. http://gath-eringvillage.world/wp-content/uploads/2016/11/OnIntegrity.pdf.

CHAPTER 3

RECOGNIZING WHAT'S REALLY GOING ON

> "Things are not always what they seem; the first appearance deceives many; the intelligence of few perceives what has been carefully hidden in the recesses of the mind."
>
> – Phaedrus[6]

Years ago, I produced an event at Madison Square Garden. As you can imagine, it is a fairly big deal to work in such a large and well-regarded facility. I had flown to New York City to do a site visit and upon my arrival I met with a fellow named Mark, the executive who had arranged the contract for the facility. He was a nice and personable Alec Baldwin-type who wore dark suit.

---

6   Phaedrus. n.d. Forbes Quotes Thoughts On The Business of Life. Accessed June 11, 2021. https://www.forbes.com/quotes/7429/.

Mark informed me that he had arranged a meeting with the MSG production team so we could discuss what was needed for the event. We headed down a white-painted, cinderblock hallway, turned a corner up a stairwell, and entered a boardroom with a long conference table where they had assembled a group of eleven people, none of whom I had ever met.

They introduced themselves with their titles and their department's role in the event planning and were there to help me have a successful event. They each asked questions about what was going to happen, which I explained was simple. "We'll start at 7:30 sharp. A woman named Marcea will come out and spend a few minutes on stage welcoming people to the event and telling them what the evening will look like. Then, she will introduce the main speaker, whose name is Werner. He will speak for about seventy-five minutes, at which point Marcea will return and give some instructions for activities on the break. There will be a thirty-minute break, then Werner will come back out and speak for another twenty minutes before the evening ends."

The group understood and asked what was going to be on stage, which was a barstool, a music stand, and a small table for water and materials. They translated this to mean that I needed a stagehand to put the items out, which required a department head to supervise. Next, they asked how the stage would be lit, and I told them I would bring my own lighting technician. They let me know this was fine, but they required that I hire their house lighting guy and lighting department head to satisfy the union requirements. They asked about sound, and I shared that we would bring in our own amplification equipment and that I already had a sound technician. They had no problem with that, except I would need to pay for their sound guy and the department head, but they weren't going to do anything.

All in all, I was told that MSG would need to staff up with ten IATSE (International Alliance of Theatrical Stage Employees) members—five workers to do the job (which they weren't going to actually do) and five supervisors for each department. They estimated the cost of the union employees at around $15,000, thanked me for coming, and we adjourned.

After the meeting, a fellow named Tony with an Italian last name came up to me. He had been in the meeting as a union agent for IATSE. Tony was quite friendly, and he immediately let me know that he liked me because I "seemed like a good guy." Since he liked me, he was going to make an offer to help. He said that "all of this stuff could get very expensive, but it wasn't really necessary" and there was an alternative way to handle it if I was interested. He said, "All that goes away." Tony asked me to show up on the morning of the event with four envelopes that each contained $500 cash, give it to him, and he would "take care of it." He assured me that if I did that, I would not receive a bill from the union and that the fees I had just heard about would be covered.

In the moment, I wasn't sure what exactly was happening. On one hand, he sounded believable and sincere; on the other hand, I wondered how he could make this promise. Furthermore, if that's how it works, then why did we have that official meeting with all of those people and their uniforms, badges, and titles?

Tony was very clear. He assured me that he knew how to do this, and said it was pretty much standard procedure. He added that if I wasn't comfortable, not to worry, we could revert back to what was discussed in "da meetin'," and they would give me an invoice from the facility for ten IATSE workers.

I left the Madison Square Garden offices and went to find a pay phone (it was the late 1980s before we all had cell phones). I wanted to call Patricia Dillan, the controller of our company. Patricia was a very nice, straight-laced accounting type in her thirties who I knew pretty well. She and I got along, although we had opposite personalities—she was a bit of a goody-two-shoes, and I was a bit of a bad boy. There was a dynamic between us where she would lay down the law every so often to keep me in check. (It worked because I needed to be kept under control, especially in those days.) We had the occasional run-ins on budgets and expenses, but we also got along very well and liked one another.

When I reached her, I did my best to explain the situation, which sounded a lot worse as it came out of my mouth. The story was filled with phrases like "some guy named Tony," "four envelopes with $500 in cash," and "all that will go away." As I recanted it, it sounded like I was involved with something very sketchy or sinister.

Since it was before ATMs were everywhere, I needed Patricia to wire me $2,000. She asked, "Is this legal?"

"At this point, I am more concerned about potentially getting whacked. This may be an offer I can't refuse," I said.

She laughed cautiously, asked me to be careful, and said, "Okay, but I will need a receipt for this." I told her that I didn't think that Tony provided receipts for these kinds of transactions so she probably wouldn't be getting one.

On the morning of the event, I arrived early and as promised, Tony was there with several of his crew. He introduced me to each of them. There was his son, Tony Junior, his nephew, Anthony, his cousin, Carlo, another Tony, and a few other fellows. Many of them had the same last name—they were somehow all related. I shook hands with each of them.

Tony took me aside and asked if I had the envelopes, which I retrieved from the breast pocket of my jacket. I handed them over, he thanked me, and shook my hand again. He said, "The place is yours. If you need anything, just ask." I asked him what the gang would be doing all day and he said, "We'll just be here if you need us."

I looked over at the crew, who were perched together in the second row of seats. Each of them had a copy of *The New York Daily News* and were perusing the sports section. He added, "It would be nice if around lunch time you could bring in some Italian sandwiches for the boys' lunch."

Around lunchtime, I decided to go out and get them some Italian hero sandwiches, figuring that would be the right call for this crew. We had some equipment on the loading dock, and I asked the guy there if he would keep an eye on it. He said, "Yeah, but I can't guarantee it'll be here when you get back."

I asked him what he meant. He replied, "Let me give you an example. Last week someone delivered a piano to this dock and, wouldn't you know it, when they got back from lunch, the piano was gone. It must have happened when I went to the bathroom or when I turned my back."

He gave me a big smile, and I realized that meant he wanted me to pay him off. I gave him $100 and asked if that would cover it. He said, "I won't take my eyes off it. I guarantee it will be here when you get back."

Here it was again—proof of how to get something done in New York City. Call it a bribe, call it a payoff, call it hush money—but what you're doing is paying somebody to provide a service that is outside the normal scope of their job. In truth, it's not that guy's job to watch my equipment, but for $100 he'll make it his job.

I returned with the sandwiches, all the equipment was there on the loading dock, and Tony, Carlo, and the other Tonys were delighted with lunch and thanked me profusely. The set-up went flawlessly. They let us do what we needed and were helpful whenever asked.

I will never forget learning that things work differently in New York City. Make no mistake—I am certain that what I've described above is how things work there. It was only a matter of my understanding that and having the good judgement to get on board with the "off-the-record" system that everything seemed to work out. Had I not recognized that this was the normal arrangement and tried to do things using the system that I'm familiar with, I would've been the one who was out of touch, not them.

What I realized is that everybody knows that's how it works there. Pretty soon, I started to adjust my behavior, my way of approaching things, and my way of doing business to be successful in New York. Money talks, and if you want to get something done, you've got to "take care of people."

CHAPTER 4

CREATING
SUFFICIENCY

S carcity is an affliction that we each have in some way. It is per-
vasive. Everywhere we look, we find that there's not enough
of *something.* We wake up and start our days thinking, *I didn't
get enough sleep. There's too much work. I don't have enough time. I'm
not smart enough. I don't have enough money. I'm not thin enough.* By
the end of the day, when we finally lay our heads on our pillows,
we say to ourselves, *I didn't get enough done today.*

In paraphrasing the teachings of Buddha, Lynne Twist, my
old friend and former colleague, said, "The source of all suffering
is a lie." These pronouncements that we unconsciously whisper to
ourselves are the exact kind of lies to which Buddha is referring.
This approach to life (which we all seem to have) is embedded in
our thinking and began when we were very young. We go through

our lives longing for more or better of whatever it is we feel would make us happy. We constantly compare ourselves to others, think that their circumstances are "better" than ours, and, therefore, believe they must have better lives, which leaves us wanting more. This is both subtle and insidious.

The conclusion that more is better is not true, not even a little bit. Things and circumstances don't make people happy. Happiness is a function of accepting what you have and being grateful for it. However, this view isn't easy to keep because we relate to our circumstances as if they determine the quality of our lives.

Recently, I had a chance to reconnect and work with Lynne Twist. Lynne is an amazing woman. She has spent most of her life working on large-scale projects that are aimed at altering and impacting vital situations such as hunger (in third world countries) and the environment. She conducts fundraisers for major charities that have raised over $50 million.[7] In the process, she's had some incredible insights and discovered some important things about abundance and scarcity.

Lynne wrote a book called *The Soul of Money: Transforming Your Relationship with Money and Life.* In it, she reveals what she calls the "Lie of Scarcity," in which she cites three toxic myths:

---

7   **About Lynne Twist: "For more than 40 years, Lynne Twist has been a recognized global visionary committed to alleviating poverty, ending world hunger and supporting social justice and environmental sustainability. From working with Mother Teresa in Calcutta to the refugee camps in Ethiopia and the threatened rainforests of the Amazon, as well as guiding the philanthropy of some of the world's wealthiest families, Lynne's on-the-ground work has brought her a deep understanding of people's relationship with money. Her breadth of knowledge and experience has led her to profound insights about the social tapestry of the world and the historical landscape of the times we are living in."*

- *There is not enough. People believe, I'm not enough. It's not enough. We're going to run out. Someone's going to get left out, so I have to make sure that I have enough.* These create what Lynne calls a "deficit mentality." She illustrates this point by explaining that the U.S. is the richest and most successful country in the world, and, at the same time, it has the largest debt of any nation.

- *More is better.* This idea leads to the thought, *I've got to have more.* So, the solution is to accumulate. Whether it be money, things, experiences, or friends, the hope is, *If I get enough, I'll be satisfied.* To make this point, Lynne points to the fact that one of the fastest growing industries in the U.S. is storage. That's right—we are now building and renting boxes for all the stuff we've accumulated and will forget that we have. Yet we are insatiable about getting more. As she spoke about this, I realized that I had spent $3,000 to build a storage shed next to my garage so I could house all the stuff that we're not *currently using.* I'm not going to lie; it's filled to the brim, and I have no idea what's in it. I'm absolutely certain I'm not going use any of it.

- *That's just the way that it is.* Since there's nothing we can do about the way things are, the solution is to keep acquiring and accumulating but never really being satisfied or fulfilled.

Lynne shared this remarkable story with me. Back in the mid-'70s, she attended an event where Buckminster Fuller (aka, Bucky) was speaking. Bucky is recognized as a scientist, inventor, and a world-renowned thinker. (For example, he invented the electric car in the 1940s, among other achievements.) At this event, he said, "Humanity has recently passed a critical threshold; and that threshold allows humanity to do so much more with so much less. There's enough for everyone everywhere to have a healthy, productive life."

Bucky said that it would take humanity probably fifty years to come to that realization and actualize it. I hope to God he was right because forty-some years later it does not look like we have gotten the message. We live in a world rooted in scarcity but where it is possible to live in a world of sufficiency. For that to become reality, humanity would need to make the shift from a "you OR me" world to a "you AND me" world. Let's face it, that begins with you and me and will require courage and boldness because we would have to see our "enoughness." This shift would lead to sufficiency, wholeness, and infinite capacity.

Lynne went on to say that "sufficiency is precise." It means that we are met by the universe with exactly what we need when we need it. It's not an amount—it's just what we need. The never-ending chase for more is not satisfying because, no matter what, we will see a lack and will want more. True abundance is enough.

Lynne continued by saying "what you appreciate, appreciates." What that looks like in practice is gratitude, thankfulness, and thanksgiving.

I make a daily practice of being grateful for what I have. I'm certainly not rich, nor am I poor, but I do have enough—in fact, I have more than enough. There are plenty of people who do not. I made a commitment that by the end of that year I would have gotten rid of anything that is not being used, worn, or enjoyed, and I would make it available to someone who would make use of it. I recently shared with a group that I chose to give up alcohol fourteen years ago, yet I have a wine refrigerator that contains about one hundred bottles of premium red wines. I don't drink red wine, and my wife only drinks white wine. So, when a guest comes over, we open a bottle of what's now a finely aged wine. They are almost always hesitant to allow us to open it until they understand that we have it for the very purpose of sharing it. We're not saving the wine refrigerator.

The day after meeting with Lynne, I shared what she had said with a colleague. As he listened, he was flabbergasted and immediately told with me that he had three storage facilities located the country. His bill for these three facilities was $8,500 a year. There's nothing in any of those containers that he's ever going to use again, but he couldn't face the thought of getting rid of all his junk.

When I asked him why was keeping all of that stuff, he replied that he didn't know what else to do. He'd paid a lot of money for some of it and some of it was his father's (who is deceased), and he thought he was just supposed to keep it all. He joked about having someone open up the units with signs saying, "HELP YOURSELF!" I bet him they would be empty within a day of posting the signs because people know that they can't get enough, and more is better. Scarcity is a strange affliction.

> *"Sufficiency isn't two steps up from poverty or one step short of abundance. It isn't a measure of barely enough or more than enough. Sufficiency isn't an amount at all. It is an experience, a context we generate, a declaration, a knowing that there is enough, and that we are enough."*
>
> —BRENÉ BROWN

CHAPTER 5

TAKE THE HIGH ROAD

Each of us has to deal with upsetting news, whether it be about a job or business situation, a health concern (yours or someone else's), or the ending of a relationship. It almost always involves emotional pain, and it feels very personal.

As a result, we often don't take bad news very well. In fact, we regularly act out our emotions in a negative and immature manner. Many times, throughout my life, I have left or ended a relationship in a messy fashion, and I usually end up regretting how I handled the situation.

I'd like to suggest that it is entirely possible to deal with bad news in another other way—by being gracious. This is easier said than done, but it IS possible. Being gracious in the face of bad news is counterintuitive for most people, and it certainly has been for me in many situations. I have learned to do it from seeing others practice it, and each time I do so, I am left happier, more satisfied, and at peace.

Often, when we are presented with a negative situation, it triggers strong emotions—anger, hurt, fear. The automatic response is to react, with the default being that almost everyone loses their cool. It sure seems like telling them off, storming out, and slamming the door would feel good, but we shouldn't do that, even if they deserve it. It is so tempting to end a relationship in that way, so that you feel like you "showed" them but that is nothing more than a reflex. It never works in your favor. You might experience resentment afterward, and it is natural to feel that way sometimes. A good friend of mine told me once that holding on to resentment is like drinking poison and hoping the other person dies. Resist the temptation to burn your bridges. Instead, let's look at an example of how it might work to operate by being gracious in the face of disappointment or a setback.

Stephanie is my daughter-in-law and the mother of my granddaughters, Genevieve and Avalon. She has spent her career in cosmetics working in high-end department stores. She started out working for Nordstrom for five years, then she moved to working for Tom Ford's signature store on Rodeo Drive in Beverly Hills.

Stephanie is excellent at what she does, and when this became obvious at Tom Ford, the company asked her to take a special position at Neiman Marcus's Tom Ford counter in Beverly Hills working as a representative salesperson. Of course, she excelled and was happy at the Beverly Hills location for four years.

Then the Covid-19 pandemic came along, which had a huge impact on retail stores and nearly crippled sales for quite some time. The store was closed for a solid two months, and even when it reopened, it did so on a limited basis, restricting customers and using half the staff.

Stephanie worked from home, but as the Covid numbers shot up in California, the retail situation grew darker. Like every department store did, Neiman Marcus's began layoffs, and Stephanie wasn't sure she would survive the cut. Eventually, the dreaded call came, and the managers informed her that her position was going to be eliminated.

Like it would be for anyone in her situation—though not surprising—this was devastating news for Stephanie. It would have a huge impact on her ability to provide for her children, and there was no certainty that she would be able to find another job doing what she loved, given that all of the stores were reducing staff. Nevertheless, she held it together during that call. She stayed cheerful and assured them that she understood completely. Instead of focusing on her dilemma, she used the opportunity to let the managers know that she was appreciative and that it had been both an honor and a privilege to work at that store and be part of their team. She let them know that she had no hard feelings whatsoever and thanked them for the great experience she had there. The two managers expressed similar feelings.

Stephanie's life had just changed dramatically, and she wasn't sure what the future would hold. Fortunately, she was given two months' severance. That amount would certainly provide a cushion for a short time, but after that, everything was up in the air. Both her income and the health benefits for her and her kids would end in sixty days. She didn't know what she was going to do next, especially with almost no retail opportunities available in the near future. The situation was both daunting and depressing. Nevertheless, she kept her spirits up, knowing that she would find a new career opportunity.

Not long after that, she was heading up the coast with the kids to visit her brother in Ojai. The phone rang, and it was her former manager. Though she was still on the payroll (she was still within her two-month window of severance pay), and therefore, still an employee, her manager told her that there had been a change and wanted to know if she would be around the following day in case they needed to reach her.

Sure enough, she got a call the next day. Her mangers had made some adjustments and had an offer for her to continue working at the store repping a different product line, which also happened to be their top-selling line. They told her that the way she had handled the "termination conversation" had impressed them to a degree that they realized that they could not afford to lose such a great employee and human being. They also said that who she was on that call was exactly the kind of person they wanted working for Neiman Marcus, and they offered her a position managing the counter for this popular line in the Beverly Hills store. This would not only restore her employment, but she would also be promoted to business manager.

This was incredible news, and no one would have predicted it, much less expected it. Soon, the store reopened, and Stephanie is now doing fine. Her positive attitude, professionalism, and behavior were rewarded, as they should be. Who wouldn't want someone like Stephanie on their team?

The first thing to know is it's not personal—it is just what is happening. It is not being done *to* you. The second thing to know is if you stay present and deal with the reality of the situation, you will find that you have more power to deal with it.

The third thing to know is "this will pass"—things will change, they always do. Lastly, you don't know what the future holds and how this will turn out—it may be the best thing that could happen, though it may not seem that way in the moment. The pastor at our church would say "that door closed so another could open." However, that wisdom is usually not present when hearing that the door has been closed.

Here is another example. My father, who was eighty-two at the time, received the worst news anyone could probably ever receive. Earlier in his seventies, he had been through a heart attack and a quadruple bypass, which saved him, but his quality of life and his spirit were greatly affected. He had been a vivacious and energetic man all his life. Now, he hung in there but needed a cane to get around and was much less active.

Eventually he suffered another heart attack on the examination table at his doctor's office. Fortunately, there was a hospital right across the street and he was rushed over and stabilized. They kept him for tests for a few days.

On hearing the news, I flew out to Southern California to see him. I was visiting him at the hospital when the doctor came in. He said he had some difficult news—my father said, "Let's hear it," and held my mother's hand. I think he knew what was coming. The doctor told him that he had stage 4 lung cancer and that he probably had less than six months left to live.

That moment is etched in my brain. Without skipping a beat, he turned to my mother and with the most loving, happy look on his face, he said, "We sure had a great life, didn't we?" That was how he felt—grateful and blessed. I know very few people who would react that way to such horrible news. My father was a great man; he taught me a lot about life, and that day was no exception. Since then, I have looked at life with gratefulness.

These examples highlight how two people handled negativity in a remarkable manner—by fully accepting the situation and the cards they were dealt. They didn't become victims, and they didn't feel sorry for themselves. Instead, they expressed gratitude and recognized their blessings.

I received a gift of a short book entitled *If God Had Meant for Man to Fly, He Would Have Given Him Wings or Up to Your Ass in Aphorisms* by Werner Erhard. There is a quote in it that says, "Happiness is a function of accepting what is." Whenever I find myself feeling unhappy, I *SWERVE* and look to accept life the way it is on life's terms.

CHAPTER 6

THE BENEFITS OF COACHING

Years ago, I was leading a transformational course in what is now my hometown of Houston. There were about one hundred attendees, and at the time, I was obsessed with golf. I played whenever there was opportunity.

In this course, I shared how passion can drive one to action, and I used my passion for golf as a metaphor for life. On our final day, a participant named Carol came up to me during one of the breaks. She was a tall, older lady with bobbed blonde hair and a pleasant demeanor. She told me that she had enjoyed my references to golf that she shared my passion for the sport. She asked if I was free the next day to play a round as her guest at her home course, TPC at The Woodlands, where she was a member.

Though I thoroughly loved the game, I was still quite a novice. and I wasn't very good at it. I expressed my hesitancy, and she immediately fed back to me some of the advice I had given that day about taking risks. She had a good case, and it was hard to argue with my own words, so I accepted her invitation.

The next day I arrived early for the round, hoping I would get to warm up a bit. Upon arriving, I told the attendant that I had an eleven o'clock tee time with a woman named Carol Mann. He immediately knew who she was and took my bag over to a cart that already had another bag on it, which was hers. Her bag had her name emblazoned in large letters along the side panel of the golf bag with the Wilson logo. On the seat of the golf cart was a stack of four dozen golf balls, with her name stamped on each ball.

Just then, the starter came to greet me and asked, "Are you Kevin? You're playing with Carol today—she'll be right down; she's getting you some cold drinks for your round." I was curious about the bag and the balls, and I asked the starter if Carol worked for Wilson Sporting Goods, which would explain the fancy golf gear. He smiled and said, "You don't know who she is do you?"

"Not really, we just met in a seminar over the weekend."

"She is one of the few women in the LPGA Hall of Fame. You are playing golf today with a legend in the sport," he said.

"Seriously?" I asked.

"I'm dead serious, bud. She is going to kick your ass out there," he responded with a big Texas grin.

I had no idea why, but I felt a very uncomfortable feeling come over me.

Just then, Carol arrived with a cooler filled with iced tea and bottled water. With a big smile and enthusiastic tone she said,

"Look at this weather! We picked a perfect day! I'm so glad you could make it!"

I told her I had just found out who she was and asked her why she didn't tell me. I said, "Carol, I know I talked a lot about golf in the course, but the truth is I'm not very good."

She replied, "Relax, we're out here today to have fun and that's exactly what we are going to do. Look, you have been my coach for the last three days and I would like to be your coach today."

I was both honored and taken aback at the same time—I wasn't sure how to respond. Of course, I said yes. So, we headed for the first tee.

As we prepared to play, a small crowd of people from the clubhouse came to watch the "pros" tee off. I was so nervous and self-conscious; I remember saying a prayer to God, asking that this drive be respectable enough to get off the tee without too much embarrassment. Luckily, I hit it square, and the tee shot travelled about 250 yards into the middle of the fairway—far beyond my expectations. Carol stepped up and hit from the men's tee with me, as any pro would, and hit a similar shot right out there; our shots ended up pretty close to one another.

We took off and headed out to the fairway to hit our second shots. I told her on the way that the biggest challenge I had as a golfer was not my swing but what goes on with me mentally while I am standing over the ball to execute a swing. I told her I would love to learn what goes through her head as she approaches and makes a shot. She agreed to share her process.

When we arrived at my ball, I estimated I was about 225 yards out (which meant a 3-wood), so I grabbed my club and headed for the ball. Carol watched as I stood over it and asked me to pause for a moment. She said that she had developed a pre-shot routine over the years, which involved standing back, looking at the hole, and imagining the flight of the ball heading right toward the hole. Next, she would take three practice swings focused on "feeling the clubhead," then she would address the ball, and check her balance on her feet. She said, "Right before I make my shot, I'll tell you exactly what I'm thinking. I select a dimple on the golf ball that I want to make solid contact with the clubface."

I wasn't sure I heard her correctly—did she actually mean that? There are 352 dimples on a golf ball, and I believe I just heard an LPGA Hall of Fame professional tell me that her focus is on 1/352 on that ball.

I looked up and said, "Are you serious? You literally aim for a dimple?"

Carol smiled back and replied, "Yes, and I want you to do that now."

I blurted out, "Well, no wonder you're so good! I'm just trying to hit the ball and you're laser focused on something the size of a grain of sand!" She laughed and responded that you must have a whole other level of precision if you want to achieve excellence.

Still a bit shocked, I addressed the ball, and did exactly as she said—I selected a dimple and imagined hitting the dimple with the clubface. I made a smooth swing, and, to my amazement, the ball traveled straight as an arrow toward the flag and ended up on the green about twelve feet from the hole (which was an amazingly rare shot for me). Carol applauded from the cart. I couldn't believe it. She took her shot, which of course was excellent, and then it took me three putts to get into the hole, but I did par the hole. We headed for the next hole, which was a par four, and made our tee shots. I hit a decent driver shot, about 220 yards, and Carol out-drove me by about sixteen yards. When we got out to my ball, she said, "Okay, do your routine, and I'll tell you the next thing. First I select a dimple, and now I select a groove on the clubface that I want to hit that dimple."

I looked up at her in astonishment again. I replied, "It's like you're pinpointing the shot."

She replied, "Exactly. Ben Hogan said that golf is a game of "MISS-management". You're not going to hit perfect shots, so what you want to do is narrow and contain the percentage that you're going to miss. I'm a better golfer than you because I miss less than you. If I hit to the right, it's only going to be a few feet, whereas yours might be several yards. This puts me in position to score better, and that's what I want you to learn today—how to manage your misses."

It made all the sense in the world. When we finished the day, I was beaming because I had discovered some things I'd never even imagined through the privilege of direct access to the mind of a golf master.

Over the next few months, my total score dropped by ten strokes—which is a big deal in golf. I had never broken ninety as a total score, and now I was doing that with some regularity. I credit that to the things I learned from Carol on that early fall day.

The benefit of learning from someone who is a master is invaluable. What you can learn in an hour can save you years of struggle and effort. Masters look at things from a different perspective—they look at it from the solution rather than the problem; they look at it from how to succeed rather than why it's so difficult.

In my own consulting practice, I do this with executives on a regular basis. I listen to their challenges (i.e., the problems they're facing), and I look at it from the angle of: "What's the desired outcome or goal?" Quite often, my clients are mired in the problem and the circumstances.

Here's an example: recently, an executive in a Fortune 100 company was sitting across from me in a coaching session. He was dealing with some frustration, so I asked him to tell me about it. His company's stock price had dropped significantly, largely due to the Covid-19 pandemic, and the company was instituting a hiring freeze. Although the business had grown over that time, the organization was reducing its headcount, so he wasn't able to hire the number of people that he needed to address the workload. He also had three people retire and he was unable to fill these spots.

This particular client worked on the accounting side of the business, and as people in finance often do, he looks at things linearly. I asked him if he was willing to look at the problem a different way.

"Did the people in those three positions do what I would call 'fungible' or 'commodity'-type work? In other words, routine functions like data entry or ledger entry?"

He responded positively.

I continued, "Well, what would prevent you from outsourcing the routine tasks and having someone manage that? In other words, it's clear you can't challenge the hiring freeze, and you can't hire a permanent staff position, but that doesn't mean you can't contract out some of the more mundane work. That's pretty much how they handled downsizing in the 90s."

He looked up at me and said, "I never even considered that."

This is a really smart guy, but he was so buried in the problem and thwarted by the "no-hire" mandate that he couldn't see past it. What was the difference between my way of thinking and his? My thinking focused on solving the problem and producing the result; his thinking was about the problem and how it stops him from progressing.

The beauty of having a coach is that he or she can look at a situation from a whole different perspective. The coach can bring context and perspective to the situation that you just can't see when you're down in the weeds. I have learned that whenever I want to excel at something, I should find somebody who's done all of the journeyman work and understands what it takes to excel.

This is the value of coaching. Coaching is helpful, not just in the business arena. Look at my golf game! Think about what areas of your life—personal and professional—would benefit from you having a coach.

CHAPTER 7

DISCOVERING WHAT REAL CHARITY IS

Wisdom from Mother Teresa

Several years ago, I decided to make a career change: I wanted to switch from delivering public transformational education courses to transformational business consulting. Before I made the shift, I decided to take a sabbatical for about a year. During that year, I was going to research, study, explore, and delve into as many fields as possible to broaden my horizons and see the world from a different perspective.

I read, studied, took classes, meditated, and traveled. One of the places I went to was India. If you've never been there, you should go—it'll change your life. While I was there, I had the profound privilege of doing something that I'd always wanted to do—service work for Mother Teresa and the Missionaries of Charity.

When I arrived in Calcutta, I set out to find the convent where Mother Teresa worked and, after some careful sleuthing (this was before the Internet), I was able to ascertain the location of her convent. I took a taxi there and knocked on the big, yellow, wall-like door that guarded the convent. A nun came to the door, and I politely told her, "I'm here visiting from the United States, and I would like to volunteer for some service work while I'm here."

She told me some of the things that the convent needed, and I agreed to do some of them. Then I asked if it was possible to meet Mother Teresa. The nun responded, "Mother Teresa never says no to anyone—if you would like to meet her, she will be here tomorrow morning at 6 a.m. for mass. If you come, she will say hello to you afterwards."

It was hard to believe that it would be that simple, but I did as I was told. I got up early the following morning and headed back with the small group of people. We were directed to go into a large room and arrived just before mass began. As we entered, we were looking at the backs of a sea of nuns. There were probably seventy, all kneeling on the cold cement floor and wearing white habits with blue stripes.

They had us sit in the back of the room; I sat on the floor next to my friend Tom. As I looked around, there was an older nun sitting in a chair. When I looked up at her face, I couldn't believe it—I was actually sitting inches away from Mother Teresa.

I elbowed Tom and gestured with my hand, mouthing, "That's her!" I'll never forget Tom's look of amazement. When mass ended, we headed out the door and Mother Teresa asked us to wait because she had an interview with an Argentine television network. The interview lasted about ten minutes, and then she was free to talk.

She came over holding a couple of prayer books and a rosary. She told me about her dream from the night before in which she'd died and gone to heaven. When she got to the gate, she asked St. Peter where the slums were because she knew that was where she'd go to work. St. Peter told her, "There are no slums in heaven."

I laughed and said, "So you'd better stick around down here for a while," which I thought was kind of funny.

She took one of the prayer books and hit me with it, saying with that stern nun-like tone, "You need to pray more!"

I promised that I would. Then she wanted to ask me a question.

"While you've been in India, have you given any money to beggars?" I responded that I had. In India, you see a lot of beggars—many of whom are children—and it's only natural that you want to help them out as much as you can.

Mother Teresa said, "I want you to make a promise that you will stop doing that (giving to beggars) and that you'll never do it again."

Her comment surprised me. After all, I was standing in the presence of a "living saint," literally the person who founded the Sisters of Charity.

I said to her, "Of all the people in the world to tell me not to be charitable, I wouldn't have expected it to come from you."

She looked at me intensely and said, "What you're doing is not charity, [it is] more like cruelty. The money you give to children does not go to them; they are slaves that are owned by a syndicate that sends them out every day to get money and bring it back. They are cruel to the children. They beat the children. And in some cases, they disfigure the children so that their begging will be more productive. When you give money to those people, you are funding the next generation of poverty in India. It's my job to end it with this generation. So, will you promise?"

I said yes. To this day, I have not given any more money to beggars.

Now, I was taught to be charitable, and quite frankly, it makes me feel good to contribute where and when I can. So, what have I done since? I've found reputable organizations that contribute to deserving, unfortunate people in situations where a helping hand will really make a difference. For example, I donate to the Shriners Hospitals for Children, the March of Dimes, 4ocean, the Society for the Prevention of Cruelty to Animals (SPCA), and other worthy causes. I invite you to do the same—after all, this advice came from a saint.

My conversation with Mother Teresa taught me that you can make a difference, but it's very important that you be particular about where you focus your efforts. What looks like charity may not be charity at all. If you're going to contribute, do some research and find out how your contribution will actually assist or make a difference. There is a list of charitable organizations at the back of this book that are legitimate and do make a difference.

CHAPTER 8

VALUABLE MISTAKES

Nobody's perfect. Everyone makes mistakes; it's part of life. While nobody likes making mistakes, they are not necessarily a bad thing. In fact, they can be the best learning experiences you can have. But for the most part, we try to avoid making mistakes. Why? Because when we fail, we experience pain.

Pain is a remarkable driving force in our lives. According to the science of Neuro-Linguistic Programming (NLP), our brains are wired to focus 80 percent on avoiding pain and 20 percent on moving toward pleasure.[8] We automatically approach the situations in our lives out of fear of what could go wrong. Our background conversations and attention are on, "What's the danger here?" That question leaves us trying to avoid making mistakes so

---

8   Brunson, Russell. "The Shift: Moving Away From Pain." The Marketing Secrets Show. March 25, 2020. https://podbay.fm/p/the-marketing-secrets-show/e/1585123200.

we can also avoid the shame, embarrassment, and pain that comes with those mistakes. So, we attempt to strategize ways around it.

But the truth is, it's impossible to avoid making mistakes. Carl Jung once said, "What we resist, persists." The more you try to avoid making mistakes, the more likely you will make them. You may be better off doing your best and dealing with the mistakes if and when they happen.

There are some very famous and successful people in history who failed miserably many times over. Almost everyone can name the man that invented the light bulb; Thomas Edison was one of the most successful innovators in American history. He was the "Wizard of Menlo Park," a larger-than-life hero who seemed almost magical for the way he snatched ideas from thin air.

It's a pretty well-known fact that more than 10,000 of his experiments failed, but Edison didn't dwell on them. It's been said, "Edison's not a guy who looks back. Even for his biggest failures, he didn't spend a lot of time wringing his hands and saying, 'Oh my God, we spent a fortune on that.' He said, 'We had fun spending it.'"[9]

Abraham Lincoln also failed at many things before becoming president. In 1831, Lincoln failed in business; in 1832, he was defeated for state legislator; in 1833, he tried a new business and failed; in 1843, he ran for Congress, failed, and failed again in 1848; in 1855, he ran for Senate and failed; in 1856, he ran for Vice President and lost. Then, in 1860, Lincoln was elected presi-

9   Hendry, Erica R., 2013. "7 Epic Fails Brought to You By the Genius Mind of Thomas Edison." *Smithsonian Magazine.* Smithsonian Institution, November 20, 2013. https://www.smithsonianmag.com/innovation/7-epic-fails-brought-to-you-by-the-genius-mind-of-thomas-edison-180947786/.

dent of the United States. What matters is not how many times he failed, but how many times he tried again.[10]

At our firm, we let our employees know that mistakes are not only tolerated, but encouraged, especially from new employees who are trying to make a good impression. At the same time, we motivate them to learn from their mistakes and not repeat them. Although it's painful to make an error, it's ultimately more painful not to make one.

Use the lesson to make a difference. And don't repeat it. Go ahead and make the next mistake instead.

10   "Lincoln's 'Failures'?" Abrahamlincolnonline.Org. 2018. Accessed June 11, 2021. http://www.abrahamlincolnonline.org/lincoln/education/failures.htm.

CHAPTER 9

ZIP YOUR LIP

Early on in my career as a business consultant, it became clear to me that really what we do in organizations is *talk*. I discovered through practical, everyday situations that what's really at the heart and soul of an organization is "a set of conversations."

Said differently, what is constantly happening in any organization are conversations at every level and with everybody—for example, executives talking to the board of directors, managers talking to employees, employees talking to customers, and suppliers talking to buyers. Both the quality of these conversations and which ones are taking place largely determine the commitments of an organization, and therefore, its results.

These discussions are what drives thinking, strategy, and decision-making. In fact, you could say that we are paid to have these kinds of talks. Since the quality of these exchanges is what determines the actions to be taken, it makes sense to conclude that the higher the level of a conversation, the more value added to the business.

For instance, if we're "just chatting," we will not likely discuss anything that makes any change or contribution to the organization. If we are having conversations about what our business is up to, we will have an entirely different level of exchange—one that potentially adds value.

Conversations take place prior to the initiation of action. Whether the company moves forward on a capital investment is a function of the dialogue that took place before that decision was made. Whether to staff up or staff down is proceeded by a discussion. Whether or not a company competes in certain markets is the result of these kinds of conversations.

There are two main parties in every verbal exchange—speakers and listeners. Typically, you'll find that people favor avoiding difficult conversations. I like to encourage people to speak up, get things on the table, and not ignore the elephant in the room. By saying exactly what's on your mind, you'll allow issues and concerns to be dealt with in an open manner. We have found that when people are willing to talk about the issues, including critical or difficult ones, better decisions get made, and more effective actions take place. This kind of open communication breeds success in organizations.

However, there are some conversations that are not productive and do not move things forward. Saying what's on your mind is not always the right thing to do. In many cases, you would be better off keeping it to yourself because it is not going to move things forward; in fact, it serves to do exactly the opposite and shuts down the conversation. I've seen this happen over and over again. When this is the case, I suggest that you zip your lip and instead take a deep breath, let the cosmic energy flow through you, grasshopper, because what you're about to say is only going to cause problems. I often find in those situations that the best course of action is to say nothing. The adage silence is golden holds true.

For example, let's say you have a negative attitude from past experiences with the IT department in your company, and there's a discussion about turning something over to IT. Here's your chance to take your well-deserved dig at IT one more time so that you can be right again with "I hope we don't run into the typical problem we always have with IT." Don't do it—it's not going to make a difference and will only do damage in the relationship. Instead of building trust, it will destroy it. When in doubt about saying something, here are three questions to ask yourself:

1. Does it need to be said?
2. Does it need to be said now?
3. Does it need to be said by me?

What I've observed while working in many organizations over the years is that these conversations, which I'll call "conversations for no possibility," are usually had by certain people who I consider "naysayers." These are the glass-is-half-empty folks who look at a situation negatively and focus on the flaws.

Such people and conversations serve to slow progress down or stop it altogether. I've seen these naysayers raise their hand right when we're about to make an important decision and lob in a non sequitur. It's usually in the form of a question that sounds something like, "Do we know what business we're really in?" or "We tried this before unsuccessfully. What makes us think we can do it this time?" Once they do this, what was a previously focused, positive conversation steadily advancing the ball is now completely thrown off track by this "psychic bong hit." It throws the conversation into a whole other gear and creates a kind of dizziness in the room. My assessment is that though these people consider themselves fundamentally committed to making a difference, instead of their contribution serving to forward the action, it derails and sends it off in a different direction, which is almost always non-productive. It leaves the other people in the conversation with questions and doubts.

Because we can choose the conversations we have, my advice is that it would be best to consider what you are about to put into a conversation and ask yourself, "Is this going to forward the conversation or is it going to derail it?" If it's the latter, maybe it would be best if it didn't get added. Another way to say this is zip your lip!

CHAPTER 10

THE SWEET LIFE

Wisdom from Papaji (H.W.L. Poonja)

In 1996, I left my career in favor of changing courses and discovering what was next. My adult life to that point had consisted of working in the travel business until I became enthralled with the world of transformation.

In the mid-'70s, I was exposed to the possibility that one could alter the course of one's life by shifting their outlook and approach to it. It was an awakening for me, and this new awareness became my passion. I studied and trained myself in the fundamentals of transformation and became a competent presenter of this kind of work that was considered "new age" and part of the "me generation."

Papaji lived in the northern city of Lucknow, which is located midway between Calcutta and New Delhi. He conducted daily Satsang meetings at his home and we were headed there to attend this sacred blessing. When we arrived on a Sunday morning, we went up to the area where the Satsang normally took place. There were a few young Western women milling around who were clearly devotees of this master and Hindu saint.

The energy was very peaceful, as expected, but we noticed a sign on the door that said "No Satsang today due to cricket match." I was a bit shocked—what does cricket have to do with a Hindu saint's teaching and why would a cricket match ever interrupt it? It was ironic, confusing, and a bit hysterical all at once.

Finally, Papaji came out to greet us. He was beaming with a beautiful energy that was unmistakable. He asked some of the disciples to serve us refreshments. Out came cold fruit juice and rolled dessert balls that were made of dates, honey, and coconut. They were delicious. I had one, and just before I had a second, Papaji stopped me and held up the candy I was about to devour. He said, "It is very important that you have something sweet every day so that you taste the sweetness that life has to offer."

As this was a world-renowned guru telling me this, I took it to heart but I thought it meant that you should eat something sweet and have dessert every day. Unfortunately, I found out is that eating dessert is fattening, and I immediately started to gain weight as I "tasted the sweetness of life." I soon realized that was not what he meant.

The message's true meaning was that it is important to stop and take in the blessings of life—when you don't do that, you don't recognize them. Papaji was telling me to be grateful for the moment, to experience it fully, and to take it in. I started doing something a little different than eating M&Ms. I began to stop and be present to the miracle that life is.

What a great insight from a profound teacher of enlightenment. I'm glad Papaji was willing to come out and conduct an informal Satsang outside his house instead of watching the cricket match that day. I'll never forget the privilege of spending time with him.

CHAPTER 11

YOUR CALENDAR IS ONE OF YOUR BEST TOOLS

P eople often say they have "too much to do." There's more to do than you could possibly ever get done. However, consider this—"you're only going to do what you're going to do today."

That sounds obvious, but most people don't relate their tasks with that saying in mind. Their to-do lists are full of things they think they should do or have to do, and they think that if they have it on the list, they'll get to it. You're not going to do all the things you *have* to do just because it's on a list. You're really only going to do what you actually do.

The key to being effective in your work is knowing that actions take place in time. Anything you're going to do takes a certain amount of time; therefore, if it's not on your calendar, it's not going to get done, and it won't happen. What's on the calendar has the highest likelihood of getting done, providing you are using your calendar.

Using your calendar is essential to getting things done. Plan and schedule the things you're committed to doing. There should be a distinction from the things you want to do, should do, and have to do. When you give up the fantasy of the unending list of tasks, you've taken a powerful step forward in productivity. Being selective and rigorous about what goes into your calendar is fundamental.

I am impeccable about my calendar. Given what's on my plate, I have to be. Therefore, I have a practice in place: I schedule what I'm going to do, and I give myself enough time to get it done. For example, I have a meeting at 10:00 AM downtown. On my calendar is "9:15–9:30 pre-meeting briefing," "9:30–10:00 drive time to meeting" (it only takes fifteen minutes to get there), "10:00–11:00 attend and participate in meeting," "11:00–11:30 drive back to office," and "11:30–11:45 debrief meeting." Having things set up this way gives me the time to (1) be briefed, (2) travel, (3) be seated (as opposed to rushing in at the last moment), (4) participate fully in the meeting, (5) return to the office and debrief my notes from the meeting, and (6) send a follow-up to the client. So, while I am only going to a one-hour meeting, in *actual* time it takes two and a half hours to complete everything that concerns that meeting.

I have been to thousands of meetings at hundreds of companies. More than half of those meetings start late, and people come in unprepared because they usually didn't allow themselves enough time to get to the meeting. The result is that they waste others' time, and the meetings are ineffective. Your time is precious, and their time is precious. You get paid to produce results with your time. Managing your time with your calendar is a valuable aptitude that will make you more effective and productive. It is an essential skill for any manager and anyone who intends to be a leader. Since you're only going to do what you're going to do in a given timeframe, putting it on your calendar increases your chances of success.

CHAPTER 12

NO NEWS
IS GOOD NEWS

L ocated in the San Gabriel Valley area of Los Angeles County is Alhambra, a small suburb where I grew up. At the time it had population of about 60,000 people and was a wonderful place to live. It was clean, safe, and beautiful with its dramatic mountain backdrop that eventually ends at California's coastal beaches.

There is a special place nearby known as the Los Angeles County Arboretum and Botanic Garden, which is available to the public and definitely worth visiting. The Arboretum is a special 127-acre botanical garden and historical site with a treasure trove of lush plants, gardens, and jungle-like settings throughout the property. Hundreds of movies and television shows were filmed there, ranging from the *Tarzan* movies in the '30s and '40s to *Fantasy Island, Mission Impossible,* and *Wonder Woman.*

When you arrive at this hidden treasure, the first thing you may notice is the loud, piercing screeches of the many peacocks that grace the property. These pheasant-related fowl were originally introduced to the property in the 1800s and have thrived there, living on the land in healthy numbers.

Without a doubt, peacocks are one of the most distinctive and exotic birds; their beautiful colors and the grandeur of their wings is unlike any other. To see the male peacock with his full display of fanned feathers in its dramatic pattern and vibrant colors is truly a sight to behold as he struts in his resplendence.

Interestingly enough, as a youngster I learned an interesting fact about where peacocks get their vibrant colors from. One of the guides at the Arboretum shared that peacocks *eat poisonous plants* that no other animals can eat. However, instead of being poisoned, they transform the toxins into their beautiful and vibrant colors. *The peacock's plumage is a living example of turning poison into beauty.* It is one of those remarkable phenomena in nature that is unique to this curious bird.

Humans, on the other hand, are highly susceptible to toxic ingredients; they can severely threaten our health or even be fatal. It is for that reason that most consumer products, pharmaceuticals, foods, cleaning products, and petroleum derivatives come with severe label warnings and external regulations. There are countless agencies and organizations that monitor these dangerous threats to our physical health.

Oddly enough, when it comes to our mental health there are virtually no regulations over what we consume in the media. This is especially true with regard to news reporting—whether it be from newspapers, journals, social media, or especially cable news, which is the most egregious of them all.

The introduction of cable news has had a huge impact on our culture. Before it existed, most people would get their information from a combination of the daily newspaper and the evening news on one of three national networks, which briefly covered national, state, and local news. It was fairly straightforward and reliable, but more importantly, it was extremely credible. It focused on reporting facts about a particular story or event because the newscasters were trained to do only this.

My mother is ninety-four and an immigrant from Dublin, Ireland since 1953. I try to speak with her at least once a week and visit whenever possible. Obviously, Covid-19 had an impact on our visits. She is sharp as a tack, but her hearing is not great; when I call her, I have to wait until she turns down the television, which is blasting MSNBC 24/7. Then, when we talk, I often have to repeat certain words or speak a bit louder than I normal would. But this is all part of the fun—she is delightful, has a wonderful heart, and a mighty spirit.

While she is very much a warm and lovely lady, make no mistake—underneath she is a tough Irish woman, and people immediately recognize both characteristics right away. I am certain that my willingness to speak up and tell my truth is a quality I got from my mother.

I spoke to her just the other day, and shortly after the call I received the following e–mail:

Hi Kevin,

I enjoyed talking with you this morning and thank you for checking in on your mother regularly.

The first thing you said was that you were writing an article telling folks not to hear the news because it was poisoned.

This is what happened here before the call:

I got up at 6 a.m. Put on robe and slippers. Opened front door and took in the newspaper. Went to kitchen. Turned on the electric kettle, put a slice of bread in the toaster, a tea bag in a cup.

Went into each room and pulled up the shades. Back to kitchen, spread toast with butter and marmalade. Poured milk in my tea. Back to living room and placed all on the table beside the fireplace. Sat in my chair and picked up the remote to watch the news while eating my breakfast.

Then…before I pressed the button, I said a prayer. Dear Lord, please let there not be another breach of the Capitol, another policeman killed, or another mass shooting.

I was absolutely shocked at what I just did. I have lived in this country for 66 years and I never prayed before turning on the T.V. to watch the news!!!

Then you called!! It makes me sad for America.

Hope it is better tomorrow.

Love,
MOM

Now this is a note from a very strong, wise, and highly principled woman. She has lived through nine decades, which included the Great Depression, World War II, immigrating to a new country, assassinations, and plenty of other turmoil—but I have never heard her speak like that until now. What has her thinking like that? What has her filled with so much anxiety, worry, and fear? I suggest to you that she has gotten that way from watching cable news talk shows.

I remember watching an interview with Barbara Walters, who was describing what it was like training to be an anchor. She said the focus was on making sure you didn't add any inflection or feeling of opinion that the viewer could pick up. Today, we have the opposite. We have emotional outbursts, flagrant opining, and reporting those opinions as though they are facts—which they are not. This leaves us susceptible to this kind of brainwashing.

My mom likes to watch MSNBC and pretty much keeps it on most of the day, where she is "entertained" under the guise of being informed by a network that foments fear and suspicion. Just like the other cable news networks, CNN and Fox, they have to fill a twenty-four-hour program with news that will seize the attention of their viewers. They do this by sensationalizing current events and wrapping them in a negative, frightening spin.

Once they have introduced the event, which they often don't report accurately, and added in a sense of panic and doom, they bring together a panel of two to six people who will then comment and build it into a tragedy or a horror story. These are usually the same people who have the network's fundamental point of view, whether it be conservative, liberal, or ultra-liberal, and they give their opinions, which are very predictable. They keep building these stories and repeating video clips, quotes, and comments to make whatever it is they're reporting much more dramatic, significant, and frightening than it really is.

This phenomenon in the media has cost it much of its credibility. People find it hard to believe what's being reported nowadays because what's being reported is no longer credible, accurate, or trustworthy. I now refuse to participate in it.

Leading up to the 2016 election, I got very interested in politics and the presidential candidates and I started watching these networks nonstop. After a while, I noticed that I was usually upset after watching these programs. I found myself getting all worked up, while before I had been in a peaceful state.

I kept noticing this pattern—I had a Sunday morning tradition of making breakfast and sitting down to watch political commentary shows, starting with Chris Wallace, *Meet the Press*, and *Face the Nation*. After an hour or two of that programming, I noticed that I was disturbed, so I did an experiment; I woke up one Sunday morning, made breakfast, sat down, and watched *CBS Sunday Morning*, then I turned the television off and decided to read a book. I couldn't believe how peaceful and satisfying it was. I vowed to stop watching those programs, and I haven't done it in months. I began sharing my realization with other people (i.e., my clients)—many of them told me they stopped watching the news months or even years ago, because it didn't contribute in any way, shape, or form to their quality of life. In fact, it did the opposite. Most of them also refer to it as brainwashing.

Cable news is fundamentally bad for your health, bad for your psyche, and bad for your spirit. I encourage you to try this experiment. Stop watching it for a month and notice how much better you feel. I do watch local news, because it covers local events, sports, and weather—all non-toxic and not designed to get you into a frenzy of concern. Just say no to cable news.

CHAPTER 13

ADVENTURE AWAITS

Pe"People tease me all the time about how much I take time off by saying, "Do you ever work? It seems like you are always on vacation."

Yes, I work. I work a lot and I work hard when I do. My wife Janeice and I own our own transformational management consulting firm; we have been consultants for Fortune 100 companies, coached executives, provided leading-edge training in leadership development, and facilitated the building of high-performance teams. We are also very good at running a successful firm with a good reputation and steady, long-term clients.

However, and maybe more importantly, we are also good at living a balanced and fulfilling life. We realize that it is very important to take time to enjoy life by learning, exploring, and discovering—we, therefore, make a significant investment in both time and money to make sure that happens. Granted, it is a lot easier for us to do since we own our own business because it allows us to set our own schedules.

I don't waste my time with New Year's resolutions—there is way too much research and evidence showing that they rarely get fulfilled. *Forbes* states, "The statistics on how many people actually follow through and accomplish their New Year's resolutions are rather grim. Studies have shown that less than 25% of people actually stay committed to their resolutions after just 30 days, and only 8% accomplish them. Don't be part of that statistic. *This year, set goals instead of resolutions.*"[11]

I do things differently. On January 1, I print out the calendar for the upcoming year. Then, I get a yellow highlighter and begin highlighting weeks to "block off" for travel, entertainment, and fun. In other words, I am making myself unavailable to work during those weeks—I slot in things plan to do during those allotted times. I have an annual fishing trip I go on every year out of San Diego in August, I attend a three-day Dave Matthews concert at the Gorge Amphitheatre along the Columbia River in Washington, I go to Cabo each year with Janeice and our granddaughters for the week of Thanksgiving, I spend four to five different weeks during the summer at our cottage at Lake of the Woods in Ontario, Canada, and I usually take a two-week cultural trip somewhere interesting and exotic between Christmas and New Year's. That leaves a few weeks unaccounted for that I can plan something spontaneous or put that time back in my calendar and schedule work. This year, I *SWERVE*d to write this book *SWERVE*.

---

11   Prossack, Ashira. 2018. "This Year, Don't Set New Year's Resolutions." *Forbes Magazine,* December 31, 2018. https://www.forbes.com/sites/ashiraprossack1/2018/12/31/goals-not-resolutions/?sh=1cabcc723879.

A few years ago, I flew out to Los Angeles to visit a very dear family member who lived in Pacific Palisades and had been diagnosed with terminal cancer. This was my "Uncle Jimmy," who wasn't technically my blood uncle at all, but he may as well have been. I was very close to him, and we considered each other family.

As shared earlier, my parents were Irish immigrants, and we grew up in the San Gabriel Valley near Los Angeles. My parents met the Murphys (Jimmy, Sheila, and their kids, Sharon, Gary, Susan, and Sean), and our families, along with my actual Uncle Mike, Aunt Florrie, and cousins Kieron, Brian, and Maureen, all grew up together. We spent weekends together at the beach in the summer, celebrated birthdays and sacraments together, and everything else you can imagine. When I was in high school, I used to work for Uncle Jimmy, who had his own tour company; he sent people to Europe, the South Pacific, and everywhere else around the world. I first worked in the mailroom, packing and sending out travel brochures to travel agencies for the upcoming tour season. Later, I was assigned other jobs—I worked in accounting, and prepared travel documents, and at one point, Jimmy hired me to design and start up inbound tourism to the United States, which was a market the company had never been in. For that, I had to take a trip to Australia and study their "camping tours" by going on one and traveling across the country.

Working for Jimmy during that time was a brilliant education in itself—he was an excellent businessman, had impeccable integrity, was fair, and always gave people the benefit of the doubt and a chance to be great. He was my first boss, and I learned a ton from working with him and for him. In many ways, I learned all about being a good businessman, a good boss, and a good leader from Jimmy.

Our families have always kept in touch, and we still get together. When I heard about Jimmy's health, I wanted see him one last time. He was in the same house in Pacific Palisades that he had lived in since the '60s. When I showed up, it was absolutely wonderful to see everyone and give them big hugs and smiles— after all, this is my family.

After lunch I sat with Jimmy and instead of talking about himself, he was extremely interested in my business and how it was going—he loved business and was very good at it. I told him that I had left the consulting firm where I was a partner for eleven years to start my own firm, and that Janeice and I were loving it and happy working together. He was delighted and kept asking questions—he wanted to know what I liked best about it, and I told him it was the freedom and autonomy to set my own course and manage my own schedule. I told him that I blocked off a week a month to reserve for non-work and personal time to be used for travel, exploration, adventures, visiting family, etc.

He said, "Kevin, good for you! That is brilliant! Did you think of that on your own?"

I did because I realized that if I don't block off the time at the beginning of the year, it will get eaten up by everything else; but if I take it out from the start—sort of like the "pay yourself first" principle that financial planners use—it is there when I need it. I can always give it back if I want, but rarely can I get time to myself if it is not blocked off.

He said, "I'm so proud of you for seeing how important that is. Do it all now while you can, while you are young enough to do it. Climb all the mountains, sail the seas, and catch all the big fish—if you wait until you are older and retired, you will be too old to do it then. Do it now."

I got a call from my cousin Gary that night saying, "What the hell did you say to dad? He came to dinner and told us all that Kevin Cullen is the only one who understands how important it is to take time off and not be working all of the time. You guys should do what he is doing and take a week off a month." I just laughed and laughed and apologized to Gary for the bank shot he got from my visit.

I have been to well over fifty countries on six different continents. I have bareboat sailed to over sixty different tropical islands in the Caribbean and the South Pacific. Each year, we try to do a two-week "cultural trip" where we can explore the world and its people in hopes of expanding ourselves and our knowledge. For example, in the last five years, we've taken the following trips:

- To Ireland, exploring modern-day, medieval, and ancient history
- To northern Africa to visit Kenya, Tanzania, Nigeria, Rwanda, and Egypt
- To southern Africa to visit South Africa, Zimbabwe, Botswana, Namibia, and Zambia
- To Ecuador and the Galapagos Islands, where we discovered the wonders of these unique places
- To Cambodia and Vietnam to visiting ancient temples along the Mekong River

Even during the Covid-19 pandemic and all of the associated restrictions, we were still able to travel to many places. Our travel this year included:

- San Diego for a five-day fishing trip that I have been going on for decades with the same group of guys (I caught a hundred-pound bluefin tuna!)
- Spending Thanksgiving week in Los Cabos, Mexico
- Spending the week between Christmas and New Years in Los Cabos, Mexico
- Spending a week in the Bahamas on one of the outer islands
- Visiting Kauai with my granddaughters
- Spending a week in Nassau/Cat Island
- Visiting our lake cottage for several weeks in Lake of The Woods, Ontario, Canada

I bring this same concept regarding taking downtime to my executive coaching practice. When I coach an executive, one of the first things I do is ask to see their calendar. I ask them to show me their:

1. Vacation time
2. Special time with their spouse or partner for date nights, dinners out alone, etc.
3. Dedicated personal time with their kids

If it is not there—and it almost never is—I tell them that one of the "conditions of satisfaction" for me taking them on as a client is that they get each of those three items entered in their calendar and take a two-week vacation with their family within the next ninety days.

You wouldn't believe the looks I get when I say that. They almost always start by telling me it would be impossible to do, given what they have on their plate. Fortunately, my new response makes it easy: "What if you got Covid—then what would you do?"

Their reaction is usually along the lines of, "Well *that's different*, I would be too sick to go to work."

My response is, "Good. Stay healthy, and have fun in Hawaii with your family. Spend time with them so that they never forget."

A couple of years ago, I was working with a senior executive in a very large company—this guy was second in command, and he had a very significant role in the company's success. He came to me for coaching, and you could just feel his anxiety, stress, and pressure when he entered the room. He had never had a professional coach, so he was a bit skeptical. When I started delving into his personal life regarding vacations and family time, he became very defensive and resistant. I told him that I would not coach him unless our coaching was holistic, which meant having a work/life balance because if he was going to be successful the way I envisioned, he was going to be successful at having it all and modeling that for the people he was leading.

After a month, his boss, the CEO, called me in to ask me how the coaching was going with his top guy. I said it was going very well. The CEO replied that he seemed "disengaged lately," and I told him that my experience was quite the opposite. He was taking the coaching and putting it in action.

The next time I met with my client for our coaching session, I asked him why his boss thought he was not engaged. He looked at me and told me that it was probably my fault. He explained, "I normally work from six in the morning until at least seven every night, and often go out to dinner with clients two to three times a week. I haven't taken a vacation in a year and a half. I started coaching with you and the first thing I did was announce a two-week vacation to Hawaii, and then I started leaving from work at 4:30 each day."

I asked him why he was leaving so early, and he said, "You told me to go to my kid's basketball games, so I did; they asked me to coach the team, and I said yes. They practice twice a week and play games twice a week, *and* since I didn't want to be unfair, I also agreed to coach my daughter's basketball team. So, I'm basically leaving every day at 4:30."

I sat there in amazement. "I didn't tell you to sign up to coach basketball teams—what the hell were you thinking?" He smiled sheepishly and confessed to having an all-or-nothing approach to life. Fortunately, the season only had another week left and the problem would disappear soon enough.

While that was way more of a *SWERVE* than I was looking for, it changed the way this executive managed his schedule and his family life—the kids got their dad back again. By the way, it has done him a world of good, and he hasn't looked back. He recently got a big promotion and is doing better than ever! If I can do it, and if he can do it, you can, too. You just have to be willing to:

1. Commit
2. Be bold
3. Block off the time so it is only available to you
4. Plan exciting adventures

CHAPTER 14

YOU CAN'T TRANSFER WHAT YOU DON'T HAVE

You may be familiar with the adage physician, heal thyself. It refers to the notion that when you give advice, your actions must match your words. When what you say and your behavior don't match up, it's called hypocrisy. Imagine an overweight doctor telling his or her patients to lose weight to improve their health, but the patient sees the same doctor at a fast-food chain drive-through "supersizing" their meal after their appointment.

Part of our work involves educating and developing competent managers to become leaders by distinguishing what leadership really is. It is all about character and modeling that character in your actions. Leadership stands on four foundational factors:

1. Integrity
2. Authenticity
3. Being committed to something bigger than oneself
4. Being "cause" in the matter.[12]

If you think about these four factors, you can easily see how each of these become pillars for being a leader. The first factor, integrity, is pretty obvious; without it nothing works. Integrity creates a foundation of reliability and trust.

Second, authenticity has everything to do with being mindful of who you want to be—it's walking the talk. To do that you have to know your blind spots.

Third, being committed to something bigger than yourself is fundamental because if you're only concerned with your own desires, then you're not believing and demonstrating anything that people will identify with, and therefore, they will not follow you. To be a leader requires followers.

Lastly and the most challenging and sometimes difficult factor is being "cause" in the matter. That requires taking responsibility for things you probably didn't even do. Yet, if you are "cause" in the matter, then you are willing to deal with it as though whatever happens is your personal responsibility.

Effective leadership is not possible if any of these key factors are missing; it depends on all four of those legs of character being solid and intact.

---

12   *The material on the Four Foundational Factors is drawn from the "Being a Leader and the Effective Exercise of Leadership: An Ontological / Phenomenological Model" course, authored by Werner Erhard, Michael C. Jensen, Steve Zaffron and Jeri Echeverria.© 2008–2020 W. Erhard, M. Jensen, Landmark Worldwide LLC. Used with permission.*

I often see things that are inconsistent with the character of leadership. Here's a recent example. Before the State of the Union address in 2020, I was on Facebook, which I use for both entertainment and to stay connected with family and friends. As I was scrolling, I saw the following post:

> State of the Union: INAUTHENTICITY & NO INTEGRITY.
>
> Be prepared to be bamboozled newly, America.

At first, I was amused that someone took the time to warn us all. (Thank you, Chicken Little.) But when I saw who posted it, I was somewhat taken aback because I know this person and know that this person teaches others about communication. He makes a living teaching some of the same character values discussed above. Effective communication requires a certain kind of openness, and his post did not reflect openness. In fact, it reflected a very narrow conclusion before the listener heard one word of the State of the Union address.

Communication is a key factor in organizational effectiveness. Most people would agree the following approaches are critical:

1. Walking into a situation openly and without a pre-conceived conclusion
2. Fully listening to what the other person has to say
3. Not prejudging the speaker
4. Forming your own conclusion once you've heard all of the facts

The Facebook post I saw has none of this perspective. Yet the person who posted it would claim to be an expert on coaching in the area of communication. What I read was clearly the opposite of that and doesn't represent what this person espouses. It struck me that if this person could be that blind to how inconsistent his social media postings are to what he teaches—and I consider this person to be fairly aware—the same must be true for others, including myself. This person spoke their opinion, decided it was the truth, and presented as absolute truth. I suppose we're all guilty of that at some level. I chose not to add a comment to that Facebook post.

Here's what I've discovered over years of delivering transformational work in organizations. If you do not practice what you preach and if you do not walk the talk, there is no way you will be effective in delivering that character to other people. They will be able to see through the inauthenticity and will know that this is only "Do as I say, not as I do." Nobody wants to sign up for getting conned at that level. Bottom line, if you're going to preach it or teach it, start with demonstrating it for yourself before modeling it to others. Walk the talk.

CHAPTER 15

BEING EXTRAORDINARY

M ost people don't think about what it takes to be extraordinary; they consider themselves normal, which translates to "ordinary."

Who doesn't want to be normal? Interestingly, many people struggle with the notion of living up to their potential. Potential is whatever you envision for yourself in the future including what you want to accomplish and do professionally. What if one's potential is to be an extraordinary human being? Can we accomplish that kind of life, or are we so engrained in assumptions about ourselves and self-imposed restrictions that it gets in our way of success?

Perhaps being extraordinary is limited by what we see as possible and what we think we're capable of doing. If we can see that something is indeed possible, and that we are capable, that is considered potential for most people. It might also be reasonable to say we can never achieve our potential because the moment we do that "something," we'd see as yet another level to strive for.

Like the horse-drawn cart in an old movie with carrot in front of the horse to keep it moving forward, there's always more to achieve. Part of what keeps people from aspiring to be extraordinary is that our society values fitting in and going with the flow. We are drawn to being complacent, stagnant, and risk-adverse.

If you have a goal but you write it off as unattainable, then you obviously will never be able to achieve it. Most people's reach is restricted by limiting, conditioned beliefs. We've bought into notions and ideas about ourselves that are, in many cases, unexamined and completely false, yet we act as though they are real.

I know someone working in the fashion industry whom I consider to be very bright, talented, and capable. With the amount of talent that she has, there is no apparent reason she shouldn't do extremely well in this field. Yet she works in a role that is probably levels down from what she is capable of doing.

On several occasions, she has requested my coaching, and I've encouraged her to break out and create her own clothing line. She really is that talented, but says, "I'm simply not ready," "I don't want to," and "I'm not there yet."

At the same time, this person complains about being undervalued, underutilized, underappreciated, and underpaid. She never has enough money. Clearly, she doesn't see in herself what I see in her. For her to accomplish the extraordinary would mean she'd have to give up her dearly held convictions about her limits and stop playing small. For most people, that's just too frightening.

Why don't we strive for and reach our full potential? The simple answer is almost always because it's "too dangerous." It's dangerous to step all the way up and all the way out, only to possibly fail. If we don't step up, then we're not at risk—we stay safe from exposure, emotionally, psychologically, and financially. Additionally, we avoid the risk of failing.

If you talk to most people, they'll have a well-constructed illusion that allows them to blame circumstances for their level of achievement. When we attempt to go outside of our beliefs and constraints, we enter that dangerous territory. It becomes risky when we are exposed, leaving us nowhere to hide and with no one to blame, and very uncomfortable.

Life is not designed for our success or for our comfort. To reach our potential, to be extraordinary, will likely mean being uncomfortable. If we don't challenge our potential to be extraordinary, like Terry Malloy, Brando's character in *On the Waterfront*, we may be left with the illusion that "I coulda been a contenduh."

CHAPTER 16

THE CHOICE
IS YOURS

P art of my job is to keep up-to-date with current management theories, themes, and approaches. I'm always interested in what new ideas and methodologies are effective and popular because they develop and change over the years, and new ways of looking at things can be very useful.

I often visit the business section of good bookstores to see what has been published recently. About fifteen years ago, I was perusing the business section of the Barnes & Noble near my house when I came across a book called *The No Asshole Rule: Building a Civilized Workplace and Surviving One That Isn't*. That's really the name of the book and it's written by a credible author, Robert I. Sutton, PhD, who is a Professor of Business at Stanford University. In the book, he addresses a taboo topic that affects every office and workplace in the world today—corporate bullies. The title alone sparked my interest and I started reading the book in the bookstore. The first lines say:

> "When I encounter a mean-spirited person, the first thing I think is: 'Wow, what an asshole!'
>
> I bet you do, too. You might call such people bullies, creeps, jerks, weasels, tormentors, tyrants, serial slammers, despots, or unconstrained egomaniacs, but for me at least, *asshole* best captures the fear and loathing that I have for these nasty people."[13]

The first line of the introduction captured my attention, and I knew I was going to buy the book, but I couldn't help continuing reading it as I stood there. I read the book from cover to cover. Sutton went on to describe common, everyday actions that assholes use. He called these the "dirty dozen."[14] The list consisted of people who have a habit of:

- Personal insults
- Invading one's "personal territory"
- Uninvited physical contact
- Threats and intimidation, both verbal and nonverbal
- "Sarcastic jokes" and "teasing" used as insult delivery systems
- Withering e-mail flames
- Status slaps intended to humiliate their victims

---

13 Sutton, R. *The No Asshole Rule: Building a Civilized Workplace and Surviving One That Isn't.* Hachette Book Group: New York, 2007. p. 1.
14 Sutton, R. p. 10.

- Public shaming or "status degradation" rituals
- Rude interruptions
- Two-faced attacks
- Dirty looks
- Treating people as if they are invisible

When I read the list, I was initially taken aback because, at the time, there was somebody I was working with who did practically all of these things. Over time, I had endured it or learned to avoid it by navigating my way around it—in short, I was putting up with this behavior. Realizing this infuriated me. As a consultant, I know from countless studies that employees stay in organizations because they enjoy working for their direct supervisor about 75 percent of the time. Not surprisingly, in my experience 75 percent of the cases where people leave, they do so because they don't like, enjoy working for, or have any respect for their direct supervisor.[15]

This criterion is a higher priority for people than pay, benefits, or work environment. Here was a book that went into great detail about what it's like to work for one of these people, and the examples it gave made irrefutable sense about why one should get out of a situation like that.

The truth is that there are plenty of great places to work, and no one needs to put up with an asshole. So, I decided I wouldn't either. I brought it to the principals of the company and let them know that I was no longer willing to tolerate working this way,

---

15   Hyacinth, Brigette. "Employees Don't Leave Companies, They Leave Managers." LinkedIn. December 27, 2017. https://www.linkedin.com/pulse/employees-dont-leave-companies-managers-brigette-hyacinth.

being spoken to this way, being treated this way, or working in a place where anyone else was. I let them know that if the situation wasn't dealt with decisively, I planned to leave. I gave them plenty of time to resolve the situation. Mind you, for most of the time I worked there, it was very enjoyable, satisfying, and rewarding. However, over the last few years, it had deteriorated into a toxic environment, and one person in particular was spearheading this—he had to go.

After a reasonable amount of time, it became clear that, while they had made some attempts at addressing the situation, what they did was not going to be successful or effective, and I decided to leave. Financially, it probably wasn't the best decision, but when I weighed the cost of remaining against the cost of staying, there really was only one choice, so I left. I started my own company, and I have to say that at first it was frightening because I had no clients and no income. But I knew that I had made the right decision, and I stuck with it.

Let me tell you, this was the best decision I had ever made career-wise. There was a new freedom, autonomy, and self-expression available to me that I hadn't experienced for a long time. I no longer had to put up with that nonsense and could focus my talent and energy on working with great people, who began showing up almost immediately. I never looked back.

I share this because I know there are many people who put up with an unworkable situation because they don't think they have the ability or freedom to do anything about it—but they do! They can just leave. There are lots of studies about people's job satisfaction in corporate America, and you might be surprised to know that about 85 percent of people are not satisfied at work.[16] Various studies say they are "disengaged."[17] Having captivated employees is essential to the success of an organization and when an organization tolerates someone who is operating inconsistently with the vision and values of the company, it is toxic and poisonous.

In 2000, Jack Welch, who was the head of General Electric (GE) at the time, wrote a letter to the company's shareholders. In it, he talked about the breakthrough they had at GE, which, at the time, was the world's greatest company and pioneered globalization. The letter states the following:[18]

> Leadership
>
> And it's about the four "types" that represent the way we evaluate and deal with our existing leaders.
>
> Type I: shares our values; makes the numbers—sky's the limit!
>
> Type II: doesn't share the values; doesn't make the numbers—gone.
>
> Type III: shares the values; misses the numbers—typically, another chance, or two.

16   Spiegel, David. 2019. "85% Of American Workers Are Happy with Their Jobs, National Survey Shows." CNBC. April 2, 2019. https://www.cnbc.com/2019/04/01/85percent-of-us-workers-are-happy-with-their-jobs-national-survey-shows.html.

17   Managing Staff. "Why 85% of People Hate Their Jobs." Staff Squared HR. December 3, 2019. https://www.staffsquared.com/blog/why-85-of-people-hate-their-jobs/.

18   Bulk Rate. n.d. "General Electric Company e." Annualreports.Com. Accessed June 28, 2021. https://www.annualreports.com/HostedData/AnnualReportArchive/g/NYSE_GE_2000.pdf.

None of these three are tough calls, but Type IV is the toughest call of all: the manager who doesn't share the values, but delivers the numbers; the "go-to" manager, the hammer, who delivers the bacon but does it on the backs of people, often "kissing up and kicking down" during the process. This type is the toughest to part with because organizations always want to deliver—it's in the blood—and to let someone go who gets the job done is yet another unnatural act. But we have to remove these Type IVs because they have the power, by themselves, to destroy the open, informal, trust-based culture we need to win today and tomorrow.

We made our leap forward when we began removing our Type IV managers and making it clear to the entire Company why they were asked to leave—not for the usual "personal reasons" or "to pursue other opportunities," but for not sharing our values. Until an organization develops the courage to do this, people will never have full confidence that these soft values are truly real. There are undoubtedly a few Type IVs remaining, and they must be found. They must leave the Company, because their behavior weakens the trust that more than 300,000 people have in its leadership.

Arguably, at the time, Jack Welch was considered the greatest business leader in the world. He discovered what Sutton is talking about—that you cannot tolerate bullies, kiss-ups, and "kickdowns" in an organization. They destroy the culture you are trying to build. Many organizations don't know this, or they don't have the courage to get rid of the toxicity. Knowing this and working for such an organization makes one complicit in it, and if you don't do something about it or leave, you have basically signed on to be part of the problem. You don't need to work for an asshole. I recently ran across an interesting quote relating to this concept that's from Rebecca Campbell.[19]

> The world is filled with people who, no matter what you do, will, point blank, not like you. But it is also filled with those who will love you fiercely. They are your people. You are not for everyone and that's OK. Talk to the people who can hear you.
>
> Don't waste your precious time and gifts trying to convince them of your value, they won't ever want what you're selling. Don't convince them to walk alongside you. You'll be wasting both your time and theirs and will likely inflict unnecessary wounds, which will take precious time to heal. You are not for them and they are not for you; politely wave them on and continue along your way. Sharing your path with someone is a sacred gift; don't cheapen it by rolling yours in the wrong direction.
>
> Keep facing your true north.

---

19   Campbell, Rebecca. 2017. "You Are Not for Everyone." Rebecca campbell.Me. February 14, 2017. https://rebeccacampbell.me/you-are-not-for-everyone/.

CHAPTER 17

INSPIRING OTHERS THROUGH STORYTELLING

Part of a leader's responsibility is to build a powerful connection with people so that he or she can inspire them. Most leaders know the importance of this role, but only the great ones know how to do it effectively, and they make it their business to do so consistently.

Emailing, texting, memos, and missives do not reach or inspire people. Those methods of communication simply transfer data and information, give orders and instructions, or make requests. They don't reach into a person's heart and soul and therefore, they don't move them to action.

Any truly effective leader will tell you that using language to touch and inspire people is essential in leading others successfully. This happens in speeches and in conversations. Virtually every time it's done well, communication is done in face-to-face dialogue. Good storytelling is an important skillset for any leader to have.

A few years ago, I worked with a CEO of a Fortune 500 company. He shared that the most significant thing he had learned about his company's public perception was that it depended on his ability to tell a good story. During the quarterly review calls with stock analysts, he needed to be able to tell a story that they would believe in. He said that the results and background circumstances, coupled with a compelling story, would get people to see a favorable outlook for the company and invest. He told me that the job is to get people to believe the story as much as you do because when they do, the company's perceived value will go up and so will the stock price.

Executives and leaders need to develop this ability if they intend to engage and inspire their audience. It is a skill, an art, and it can be developed. Unfortunately, most of us know that storytelling is a dying art, mainly because of our increasing reliance on technology. It's no secret that people have stopped having conversations and have begun to direct their attention to a little screen in their hands.

Years ago, I was on a vacation in Ireland and visited the Aran Islands off the west coast. I took a quick jaunt on an ass-cart ride and learned about the old and treasured art of storytelling.

The ass-cart is a small cart or carriage pulled by donkeys. The salty man driving the cart explained that storytelling used to be such a strong part of their culture. If you went into anyone's home, you'd hear amazing stories of leprechauns, fairies, and other local lore from the past. This was how people learned about the life of their ancestors. But that didn't happen so much anymore. Storytelling is slowly disappearing in our culture and society because of the influx of technology—the Internet, TV, and other broadcast media. People no longer need dialogue to entertain. The art of telling stories is almost gone.

How do you develop effective storytelling? There are essentially five elements of a story:

1. *Have a central theme* that runs throughout the entire story; what is the point you want to make? Have that theme grow as the story is told and weave it throughout the conversation.

2. *Draw on your own experience.* Share real life experiences that demonstrate the point. People don't want to know how great *you* are. They want to know how this applies to them, or in other words, they want to see how great they can be.

3. *Paint a picture.* Give them details that allow them to conjure a picture in their mind. Show—don't tell. You want the audience to see themselves in your story. Embellishing the story with your experiences makes it more vivid and real.

4. *Evoke wonder.* Engage people in the telling of the story. You want them to stay on the edge of their seats, captivated and wanting to know how the story is going to turn out. As they take the journey with you, your audience will

feel they have learned it for themselves. It becomes a personalized conversation.

5. *Keep it simple.* The story should demonstrate one conflict or one lesson only.

Storytelling is an invaluable tool for any leader, and while some have a natural ability, it is a skill that can be developed with some focus and training. It's my experience that all successful leaders find a way to inspire and move others through storytelling.

CHAPTER 18

BEING A BIGGER PERSON

In life, we often get caught up in insignificant matters that really don't make any difference. Getting caught up in these things takes us off our game by being very distracting and unproductive. There's an art to living where you consistently score three-pointers because you've got your game organized to produce high scores. It takes being a bigger person in both significant and smaller matters. Being big about something is an art that requires skill and thoughtfulness.

The other day I was having lunch with a client near his place of business. After we took a quick look at the menu, the waitress came. I ordered the chicken Romano salad, which I almost always order, and my client ordered salmon with rigatoni. While we were engaged in a great conversation, the waitress came with our meals and placed the chicken Romano salad in front of me and the same salad in front of my client. There was an awkward moment while we looked down, and I said, "That doesn't look like salmon with rigatoni to me."

The waitress reached for his plate to make the correction. My client said, "No, this will be fine. It's something new and I'd like to try it."

She made another attempt, and he assured her he was satisfied with the plate that was in front of him. When she walked away, I looked at him and commented, "My god, that was amazing." He really didn't know why I thought so. I told him that "error" would have become enough of a major issue for many people to have made a big scene; I have witnessed meltdowns over much less.

He said that after I had ordered the salad, he wondered if maybe he should try it, too. We both got a laugh and I said, "You willed it here."

Given what had just happened, I continued, "I appreciate something about you, Ken, and that is your ability to be a big person and not get hooked by inconsequential things. You focus on what matters. And that's a great attribute of yours."

I have known Ken for fifteen years and have never seen him be anything but dignified and gracious, which is probably why he is so good at his job and such a strong leader. His interaction with the waitress was a perfect example of someone being a bigger person than the situation. It's easy for any of us to be small—it takes something on our part to be big about anything.

Conversely, I recently had dinner with a female client who had experience in the restaurant business. She had pretty high standards and, since this was a top-rated restaurant, she expected the highest level of service. What ensued was a series of tirades correcting the waiter and commenting that everything he did was wrong. We had ordered slowly, several times actually, because she was sure that he didn't understand what she was saying. (He did.) Additionally, she had ordered a "special appetizer" that would take a while to prepare and instructed the waiter that her Caesar salad be served before the appetizer.

Of course, the appetizer came first. The waiter couldn't have been more apologetic.

My client complained that the salad was soggy. She had ordered to split two entrées and explained three times, speaking to him like he was an idiot. She just lit into the guy and just wouldn't let it go. It was so embarrassing that I wanted to crawl under the table.

After her third "attack" on this poor guy, she turned to me and said, "Can you see why I'm single?"

She was joking, but there was a lot of truth to her comment. Even she recognized how awful she was being, and she could tell that I was uncomfortable. That prompted my request that she be nicer to the waiter for the rest of the meal because she was making me very uncomfortable. I explained to her that he was a great waiter and didn't sign up for the Michelin test.

From that point on she was very pleasant to him. She apologized, but it took my request to get her to back off and become the bigger person.

How we react and how we respond to any given situation is a choice. It takes practice and discipline to develop the trait of being the bigger person. Generally, we react in fight-or-flight mode. It's an instinctive response to protect ourselves from real or perceived threats. But after a few deep breaths, we usually discover that most of what's coming at us is not a threat at all, and we have a choice about how we'll respond.

We have an automatic response to "being right," which is something that is important to most people. Being the bigger person sometimes means that we apologize, even when we're sure we're right. It's a very generous act. At some point we need to consider what's really important—moving things forward or being right. We always have a choice of striking out with our righteousness or letting it go for the sake of what's possible. Being the bigger person makes you a better person.

CHAPTER 19

DO WHAT MAKES A DIFFERENCE

If you're like me, I'll bet you try to get the important things done first. They seem significant because there's usually a benefit in getting them done or some degree of pain for not getting them done. If you completed these tasks, then you assumed it was because they were vital. However, we often don't relate to things on our plate with any sense of urgency. We procrastinate, particularly about situations we don't want to confront.

Being effective at producing results is a direct correlation to the speed with which we move to complete things. It has been said that:

> Your power is a function of velocity, that is to say,
> your power is a function of the rate at which you
> translate intention into reality. Most of us disem-

power ourselves by finding a way to slow, impede, or make more complex than necessary the process of translating intention into reality.[20]

To do that, the task has to exist in time. Here's something I've learned that I have burned into my DNA, and it has changed everything: "If it's not on the calendar, it doesn't exist; it's not going to happen."

There is an obvious benefit for getting things done and acting with priorities, so why don't we approach things this way? There are three elements that account for our tendency to put things off. The first is having no sense of *urgency*. Certainly, there are challenges that happen in life that we resolve with speed. However, those things usually have some kind of consequence attached and the pain of not doing it is greater than the pain of doing it; consequently, we act.

Secondly, we fall in the trap of *someday*. You know those as things that we'll get to *later*. We put them things on the list of what there is "to do" and that keeps them in existence, but they exist only on the list; simply being on the list doesn't mean they will actually get our attention for action. We don't have time for those things now, and we may never get to them.

The last is *complacency*, which stops us from taking any action. There are many situations in our lives to which we have become numb. We've learned to tolerate them, even those things that we said would never tolerate.

---

20 "Human Performance Improvement Tips." n.d. Wernererhard.Com. Accessed June 28, 2021. http://www.wernererhard.com/cuttingedge.html.

There's an interesting metaphor about a frog. If you put a frog in a pot of boiling water, it will jump out of that water immediately, but if you put it in a pot of cold water, turn the burner on, and slowly increase the heat, the frog will boil to death. It will keep adjusting to the ever-slight increases in temperature that will eventually kill it.

People are sometimes like frogs. We allow ourselves to adapt to and tolerate things that don't work, even when the consequences are dire. Most people divide their tasks into two categories—what's important and what isn't. Ideally, people go to work on the tasks they've decided are important and pay less attention to the unimportant ones.

I want you to consider the possibility of a third category. It's a category that most of us don't think about because it's not important. I call it "what makes a difference." The items that fit in this category may not even fit into the first two categories. However, these items are distinct and make a big difference.

Here's an example. Recently, I was copied on an internal document from a client's company so that I would be aware of what was going on. It was about the company's core values. My client didn't ask for feedback about it, but after I read the document, I realized that there were things that I might be able to say about it that would make a difference. I asked her if she was interested in discussing the document. She said she was.

I soon shared what I thought would make a difference and some suggestions on how to make it better. She loved what I suggested, and we produced a second version of the document, which then led to a third version. The day after our call, she sent me a note thanking me for having the conversation and told me it was very valuable. Our discussion had encouraged her to act on something that would elevate that area of the organization to a new level.

Clearly, my input came from that third category—maybe the "what makes a difference" category is the most important of all.

Portions of the material in this chapter are derived from the work of Werner Erhard and Landmark Worldwide LLC and are used with permission.

CHAPTER 20

GORILLA TAXI

Wisdom from Afrika, the name of my taxi driver in Rwanda

From an early age, I was curious about the world. Without question, my favorite subjects in school were history and geography because they revealed stories and mysteries about humanity. I recall reading about the pyramids at Giza in Egypt and the life of the pharaohs. The stories about this subject left me in wonder. I dreamed of one day visiting this magical place, so it was bound to happen eventually.

Recently, I fulfilled my dream of travel on an exciting adventure to Africa. On this trip, I visited South Africa, Tanzania, Rwanda, and Egypt. If you've never been to Africa, I highly recommend it. It will change your life. While in Tanzania, we visited the Serengeti Plain and got to see all animals in their natural habitat. There are no words to describe how amazing this is to experience in person.

Next on the itinerary was Rwanda, where I discovered something both profound and simple at the same time. As you may know, a horrible genocide took place there in 1994. More than two million people were murdered in the span of about three months over tribal categories assigned by the government. This tragedy is chronicled in the acclaimed film, *Hotel Rwanda.*

I was visiting Rwanda so that I could trek into the mountains to see the mountain gorillas. It was in these mountains that Dian Fossey conducted her famous research on behalf of these precious animals. When she started her work in 1960, the mountain gorillas were in grave danger of becoming extinct due to poaching. Their population of had diminished to about 200. There are now more than 1000 gorillas and poaching has been eliminated.[21]

Despite the tragedies of the past, Rwanda is a thriving, developing, and inspiring country. The country's president, Paul Kagame, took over after the genocide and began to aggressively set the country on the right track. Under his leadership, it was able to eliminate corruption and has inspired its citizens to rebuild and grow in a unique and extraordinary way.

Kegame was able to institute some remarkable things. One of his commitments was to cleaning up the country and keeping it clean. He urged citizens to be proud of their homeland and have it be totally free of litter and waste. Now, on every last Saturday of the month, the entire country spends the morning in an activity called "Cleaning Day," in which every citizen cleans the cities, streets, fields, and the forests. Everyone is required to do

---

21   Hewitt, David. 2018. "Mountain Gorillas Moved Off 'Critically Endangered' List." Gorillas.org. November 15, 2018. https://www.gorillas.org/mountain-gorillas-moved-off-critically-endangered-list/.

this, including the president. If, for some reason, you don't participate and instead are seen driving down the street, you would get pulled over and handed a shovel or a broom and receive a small fine.

When I arrived in the capital city of Kigali, we had a three and a half hour drive up to the hotel. After hearing about this cleanliness practice, I found it hard to believe so I made it my mission to find trash on the ground as we drove through the countryside. We travelled several hundred miles through mountainous paths and brush, and in three and a half hours, over several hundred miles, I could not find one piece of trash in that country. Not one piece! This was so unbelievable that I began wondering aloud what would happen if I did a little experiment and put a piece of trash on the road. Our driver and guide on the journey, Afrika, assured me that within thirty minutes whatever I put down would be gone. He laughed and said, "You'd be wasting your time."

"How do you know?" I asked.

"Because I would pick it up! That's just the way it is in our country," he replied.

I would challenge anyone in the United States to conduct a similar experiment. I think we can agree it wouldn't go too far, as we are not structured as a society to seriously consider such a project.

This probably seems like a small thing, but I assure you, that kind of cooperation has infiltrated Rwandan culture in many extraordinary ways. First and foremost, what's apparent is the level of pride the citizens have. If you ever have a chance to visit the country, you will feel it immediately when you arrive. While on my way to see the gorillas, I learned that real transformation is possible in any circumstance if you have a leader who takes a stand for the future and provides the leadership required to bring that vision to fruition.

CHAPTER 21

MAKING TOUGH DECISIONS—NOW

Often when we become aware of a business issue, such as a bad hire or some other mistake, we put off dealing with the problem in the moment that we discover it. In hindsight, we can clearly see that when we've waited to handle these issues, they got worse. Did we think it would resolve on its own? No, of course not. It never does. So, why do we wait? What does it take to deal with something with a sense of urgency?

Everyone knows that when you deal with an issue completely, you'll feel better. You lighten up, your integrity is restored, taking action becomes easier. Things start working again when the company's core values are alive and well.

A while back, I hired the wrong person. The mistake I made was not following the process I have in place for successful hiring.

Because I knew the person, and we'd been friends for many years, I made an exception and disregarded our process. It cost a six-figure salary, and worse, well over a year's worth of productivity in our firm. It also cost us our freedom, our creativity, and our time. In my weak attempts to deal with the issue by doing everything but what I knew I had to do, I avoided it as much as possible and also didn't communicate with anyone about the problem. This is the opposite of our company's culture. Even though I knew, (and the employee knew) that I had made a bad choice, I couldn't seem to let it go. I kept trying to fix a situation that would never work. At the time, I didn't realize how much I had begun to accommodate this person's poor performance and bad work habits. After some time, I began to notice that there was a "cloudiness," and I came to the realization that it was an integrity issue.

In a previous chapter, I referenced a business philosophy that was imparted by Jack Welch, who was CEO of General Electric. He shared how GE was able to grow and thrive so dramatically by identifying four kinds of people. I applied Welch's model to this particular situation. In chapter 15, I outlined this philosophy, and here it is again:

> *Type II*: doesn't share the values; doesn't make the numbers—gone.

At some point, I became aware that the person I had hired fit into Welch's second category. They didn't share the values or produce results. They seemed to operate with an entitlement mentality—a "what's in it for me" and "what's the minimum I can do" mindset. Once I acknowledged the truth about the situation, my choice was clear. They had to go. But it took me awhile to admit it, which was a *big mistake*.

So, what is it that keeps us from making tough decisions when problems arise? Maybe hoping that there will be some imaginary force that will intervene and that the problem will solve itself. However, you and I both know that that's not going to happen. What is required is powerful and decisive action.

Running a successful business requires making tough decisions. Effective action takes honesty and courage. It's uncomfortable and hard to do, but that's what it takes. Colin Powell said, "Bad news isn't wine. It doesn't improve with age."[22]

22   Powell, Colin. n.d. "Colin Powell Quote." AZQuotes.com. Accessed June 11, 2021. https://www.azquotes.com/quote/235179.

CHAPTER 22

PROMISES
TO YOURSELF

As I said earlier, I do not make New Year's resolutions. I don't make them for the simple reason that they mostly don't work—people ultimately fail at them.

Several years ago, I read an article that provided some discouraging data about New Year's resolutions—but : that by January 22nd, 88 percent of New Year's resolutions will have already failed and been abandoned.[23]

Sadly, this didn't surprise me. Somewhere in those numbers, I had been a casualty over the years. I, too, would announce the typical statement, "This year I'm gonna..." Like many others, I

---

23   Editor. n.d. "New Year's Resolutions. . .so Easy to Break." Lehighvalley
      magazine.com. Accessed June 27, 2021. https://lehighvalleymagazine.
      com/2019/new-years-resolutions-so-easy-to-break/.

have made resolutions that have failed, and I didn't want to be part of those statistics anymore. *Yuk!*

According to *Forbes*, 40 percent of us make New Year's resolutions and only 8 percent of those resolutions get accomplished.[24] That is a pretty stark and dramatic piece of data. In light of it, I decided I would conduct an experiment to see if I could beat the odds. This wasn't a good idea to begin with, but I was hell-bent on discovering if there was a way to defy being a statistic. The first question I asked myself was: *How can I avoid failing at New Year's resolutions?*

The answer is simple and obvious—don't make them. Indeed, one foolproof way you can guarantee you will not fail at this is to not make a resolution. Bingo! So, one year I made none, and guess what? I did not fail to keep a New Year's resolution—I had a perfect score...ta-da! It may not be very impressive, but at least I didn't fail.

Still, that was not very satisfying, so the next year I asked myself a different question: *What would it take to actually make a New Year's resolution and be successful in keeping it?* Just doing this once would be a win compared to what most people do.

I decided to look at the data, which, as I have said, reveals that, in the first twenty-one days, almost everyone fails. Ah ha!— the insight came quickly—don't make any New Year's resolutions until January 22. With the odds stacked against you so heavily, why fight it?

---

24   Diamond, Dan, 2013. "Just 8% of People Achieve Their New Year's Resolutions. Here's How They Do It." Forbes Magazine, January 1, 2013. https://www.forbes.com/sites/dandiamond/2013/01/01/just-8-of-people-achieve-their-new-years-resolutions-heres-how-they-did-it/?sh=31263192596b.

A wise man once told me, "Ride the horse in the direction it is going." So, I decided that I would make some resolutions, but I would wait until January 22 and see if that helped. I also didn't want to target something that I would likely fail at, like going to the gym every day, so I picked something that I really wanted to do, that I could do, and that I felt I would benefit from.

I chose to commit myself to prayer and meditation every day. I thought I could actually *do* that. I would benefit from having a deeper spiritual relationship, and I could do it pretty much anywhere. I travel a lot, and it turns out you can pray and meditate in any country, so it was entirely doable. I started on my "grasshopper" journey to see if I could do it, daily, consistently, and make it through the year.

Since it was a simple enough task to accomplish, I knew I *could* do it. However, my biggest fear was that I would *forget* to do it, so I needed a tool to make sure I wouldn't forget. I decided to get a small bracelet of Mala beads and wear them on my right wrist. That way, at some point during the day, I would look at them and mediate, even if it was the last thing I did at the end of the day. Sometimes, I was reminded when I took the band off to get ready for bed. The result—I successfully prayed and meditated every day for a whole year.

This gave me great satisfaction on several levels. The benefits of prayer and meditation are widely known:[25]

1. They improve self-control.
2. They make you nicer.

---

25   Clay Routledge, Ph.D., "5 Scientifically Supported Benefits of Prayer." *Psychology Today.* June 2014. https://www.psychologytoday.com/blog/more-mortal/201406/5-scientifically-supported-benefits-prayer.

3. They make you more forgiving.
4. They allow you to trust.
5. They help offset negative health effects of stress.

After having accomplished a solid year of a single practice and gaining discipline in doing one thing consistently, I wanted to build on my success and use the momentum to take on more consistent practices. I became intrigued about forming habits and what it takes to create a consistent one. There have been many studies on this, but the number that seems to be consistent is twenty-one days.[26] You must perform the task or practice consistently for twenty-one days in order to form the habit.

By the way, this is also true for bad habits. As you might also imagine, I got a bit cocky with the momentum I gained in year one and I picked five new practices for the following year (after January 22, of course). Year two was not so good; I didn't write or blog each day as I had intended, my gym appearances were way below the standard, I rarely picked up the guitar to practice, I did not eat the foods I said I would, and I was hit and miss at telling one person that I loved them each day. It wasn't a total disaster because I did more of each of those things than if I had not set out to do them, but it wasn't the same—it didn't yield the blast of satisfaction and fulfillment that the first year had.

Obviously, I was curious, and I researched this further. I learned, also from studying data, that you are more likely to succeed in delivering on initiatives if you keep it to three. If you go

---

26   Popova, Maria. 2014. "How Long It Takes to Form a New Habit." Brain pickings.Org.January2,2014.https://www.brainpickings.org/2014/01/02/how-long-it-takes-to-form-a-new-habit/.

beyond that, you immediately begin to diminish the likelihood of success. (I suggest you trust me on this one, but if you don't, you are welcome to read about these studies in *The 4 Disciplines of Execution*, by Sean Covey, Chris McChesney, and Jim Huling.) I now take on three, and only three, resolutions from three different categories: (1) physical, (2) spiritual, and (3) mindfulness. And I am keeping them *doable*. This year's resolutions are:

1. a small series of daily physical routines (usually push-ups, lunges, squats and kicks)
2. learning about something each week (I read a book, listen to a podcast, take a seminar, or see a live performance), and
3. writing each day (I have committed to publishing a book in 2021).

In summary:

1. Don't make New Year's resolution(s) until January 22.
2. Start off slow.
3. Pick something simple that you really want to do.
4. Don't try to end hunger and resolve world peace on your first go.
5. Choose something that is doable and appealing to you.
6. Set up a reminder for yourself that makes it impossible to ignore.
7. Get the first twenty-one days under your belt if you want to succeed (critical).
8. Don't pick more than three things (do not violate this one).

CHAPTER 23

NOT EVERYTHING IS AS IT SEEMS

Have you ever had the shocking realization that something you believed to be true was completely false? You were absolutely sure that something was one way, then you suddenly discovered it wasn't that way at all. This certainly happens in life situations, but it also happens in business situations where decisions were made based on a wrong assumption. It could be a theory about the market, a trumped-up belief about a buyer's interest for a product or underestimating your competition. Nevertheless, you placed a bet on how you saw that situation and it turned out you were dead wrong. This can be very costly.

"Daniel-san, not everything is as seems."

– Mr. Miyagi, *The Karate Kid*

Here's an example of what I'm talking about, and while it's not a business example, it highlights what can happen when you don't see the bigger picture.

Way back when I was dating someone, early on in our relationship, we took a vacation trip to Kauai. Though a small island, Kauai has many different features, including the dramatic Napali Coast and Waimea Canyon, which is a mini-version of the Grand Canyon. The island is very peaceful, serene, and calm; there's not much commercialism, which gives it a very relaxing vibe.

One day, we went for a drive exploring the island. As we were traveling up one of the winding roads, we noticed a young couple was just coming out from a trail by the side of the road with big smiles on their faces. The trail looked interesting, so we pulled over and asked them what was down that way. They said there was a beautiful waterfall about a mile away, and if we just walked along the rocky bank of the stream, we would find it.

We parked, took our day packs and headed down the trail in search of this picturesque area. Just as they told us, after about a half a mile, we could hear the powerful rushing sound of what turned out to be an absolutely stunning waterfall. As we approached, we saw a deep blue tropical pond beneath it. We stood in silence for a moment, amazed at its beauty. We had this moment in paradise all to ourselves, and with nobody around, we decided to skinny-dip.

My girlfriend fancied herself as a bit of a hippie-goddess. This, for her, was a very sacred moment. She'd be free in nature and one with the universe. She happened to be quite attractive and particularly curvaceous. She headed out into the middle of the pond, where the mist of the waterfall sprayed in the air and floated fully naked. We spent about an hour there together.

After some romantic carrying on, we dried off, put our clothes back on, and headed back up the trail to our car. She exclaimed that this experience was one of the most extraordinary moments of her life—being alone in a private paradise and being "at one" with nature.

We drove up the mountain road about a mile and as we approached the top, we noticed there was a lookout point where five large tourist buses were parked. We were curious, thinking something must be interesting. We got out of the car and joined about one hundred Japanese tourists loaded with still and video cameras who were recording the sights below. When we peered over the rail, we saw the very pond we just left. Unbeknownst to us, during our "private, sacred time," it was now clear that hundreds of Asian tourists were capturing those moments for posterity. They documented the goddess in all her glory, naked and floating in this exotic pond.

My girlfriend's face froze. She looked as if she'd been hit with a taser. By this time, I was laughing hysterically and seeing the humor in this said, "You are now a porn star in Japan." She did not find it funny. Fortunately, this was before the internet and the explosion of YouTube, so I don't think she ever made it onto the social media scene.

Beyond the obvious, we both learned an important lesson that day. Sometimes a situation isn't how you think it *really* is. Making assumptions based on what's in the foreground, not considering what's in the background and beyond, can lead to surprising and potentially dangerous consequences. Keep your eye on the project, but step back to see the larger picture before committing your resources. Sometimes you think it's one way, but it's clearly another.

CHAPTER 24

DEFEATING OVERWHELM

Wisdom from Jack Mantos

Being overwhelmed is a situation that is familiar to everyone. There will always be many tasks for us to resolve, and it feels like the list is infinitely growing. We all know that it's not possible to get all of these tasks done, and sometimes, we begin to feel overwhelmed. In those moments, we see no way of finishing anything.

When we become overwhelmed, we are ineffective; this feeling has its own force. It becomes larger than life, halting all action. It becomes a condition in which you feel you never get anything done, and you're upset about it. You are stuck, and while you're busy being stuck, you will surely fail. It's like trying to move forward while running on a circular track.

Years ago, I was talking to a colleague of mine, Jack Mantos, and sharing frustration about all the things I had to do. I said, "I'm completely overwhelmed."

Jack, who was someone who could handle a lot of things at once. He said, "Overwhelm is a state of mind. It is not a fact, and how you get yourself out of overwhelm is by dealing with reality. There's a certain number of things you're completely capable of and comfortable with handling at a given time. Overwhelm is when you surpass your perceived threshold for carrying all of those things at once."

You can handle and manage the demand on your capacity until you reach one more unit that puts you in a state of overwhelm. For example, in the following diagram, the demand has exceeded capacity—that's when overwhelm takes over. When you're in that state, you're never going to get it all done.

What does overwhelm look like?

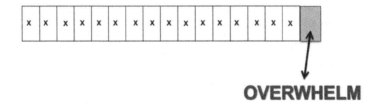

All the squares represent your total capacity
X = 1 unit of capacity

OVERWHELM

Overwhelm is to bury or drown beneath a huge mass. Before that point, your available capacity is manageable. However, when you add that one additional item, you hit overload, which puts you over the top and beyond your ability to manage the tasks at hand.

How can you be powerful when facing the state of overwhelm? What can you do to get out of that condition? American soldier Creighton Abrams once said, "When eating an elephant take one bite at a time.[27]" Everything we have to do can be broken down into manageable and finite units. Until you break mass apart into these units, you will never get anything done because you will be buried under its weight. You must either delegate some of tasks or eliminate them. It is essential to get things to a level that is confrontable.

Overwhelm is a psychological phenomenon. It is not real. The reality is that there are the tasks that you will do and those that you won't do. It's our psychology that has us believing that we have to get all of the tasks on our list done.

You need to prioritize the importance of each item and put it into your calendar in order to deal with it. When you consider the entire list of things to do, you're going to see something really interesting—there will be things you are committed to doing, and there will be things that you're really not. You may find some things you want to get to at a later time, so create a way of keeping those things in existence. You'll also find there are some things you really will never get to. Eliminate them. Keep in mind that life occurs in units of time, and you have the capacity to fill only so many of those units.

You either have to stop doing one of the things you're already doing or give away (i.e., outsource) some things. The question you need to ask yourself is: *Is it a good investment to outsource any given item?* If it is, and you find the right person to whom you can outsource, you are left with time to work on the things that you should be working on, while experiencing relief knowing that the other things are being done by someone you trust. This then leaves you stress-free, confident, and productive.

---

27   Miller, Frederic P., Agnes F. Vandome, and John McBrewster, eds. 2010. *Creighton Abrams.* Alphascript Publishing.

CHAPTER 25

STRESS-FREE LIVING

I t's no secret that stress contributes to heart problems. It can also
be linked to other issues including insomnia, eating disorders,
depression, colds and viruses, circulatory problems, systemic
or local infections, diabetes, and cancer. In today's complex and
hurried world, where we're bombarded with information, local
and national crises, and our own personal concerns, stress enters
our lives quickly and effortlessly. The more complicated your life
is, the more likely stress will become a concern for you.

Years ago, my boss introduced me to a skilled practitioner
of an Eastern medicine practice called Sugi, which is a form of
acupressure developed in Korea. His name was Dr. Choe. He
is a world-renowned healer who has treated several dignitaries,
including emperors and popes. Over the years, I got to know Dr.
Choe and, as our relationship developed, he began to visit my
home in Denver and stay with us for a week at a time. The people

who received his treatments found them remarkable. I witnessed "laying of the hands" that produced unadulterated miracles and made conditions "disappear."

Though Dr. Choe was an older man, he kept a rigorous schedule for his daily treatments—he would get started at 8 a.m and finish at 6 p.m with only a few breaks in between. We had dinner together in the evening, and we would sit in the living room talking afterward.

Dr. Choe was a wealth of knowledge and in the course of these evening chats, he imparted some insightful concepts. Once, when we were chatting about health and well-being, I was trying to understand how his work with meridians was so powerful in freeing up energy and eliminate blockages. One night, I asked: "Dr. Choe, why is it that some people eat correctly, exercise regularly, drink lots of water, and have a healthy lifestyle in general, yet they can get very sick and in some cases die in their thirties from heart failure, while others can live a life of reckless hedonism—eating bad food, smoking, drinking, and surviving on little sleep—and live to be one hundred years old?"

Dr. Choe said that the word *disease* literally means dis–ease (not at ease), which translates to worry. People who live a simple life are more at ease, less worried, and therefore experience less dis–ease and, therefore, less stress. He said that stress is the silent killer, and those who worry are prone to stress and attract disease.

Dr. Choe pointed out the obvious benefits of prayer and meditation to quiet the mind, reduce stress, and act as a catalyst for letting go of worry. He said moving the body and being in nature also help people to be less stressed and worried. He went on to explain that the practice of gratitude—being grateful for what you have and for the moment—limits the chances you will have a worried existence.

What I took away from Dr. Choe is that it would be in my best interest to eliminate or get rid of anything that I don't need. It would also be in my best interest to simplify my life and not spend my time engaged or focused on things that I don't care about.

Don't worry. Be happy, be grateful, and be free.

CHAPTER 26

BREAKING
BAD HABITS

I f you have ever been to London, you are probably aware that American tourists are often involved in serious accidents and fatalities each year while attempting to cross the street. The reason for this is simple—out of habit, they look the wrong way and then enter the crosswalk. As you also know, traffic travels in the opposite direction in the United Kingdom than it does in the United States. Americans are used to looking to the left when they are about to cross the street; this is a well-honed habit that was developed over a lifetime. Unfortunately, even though they *know* that traffic flows the other way, the habit of looking left overrides their knowledge. Instead, *their actions are dictated by a behavior pattern* that was developed over time for the situation of crossing the street. Even though they know they should look right because traffic goes the other way in London—they still look left. Why? Simply because there is a difference between knowing something and actually doing it.

You can know something intellectually and still act in a way where that information does not influence the action. Said another way—your actions are not coordinated with the situation you are in. Said even more simply, their decisions in the present come from the past; they are not present to reality.

How can this be? These are intelligent people, so why do their brains not adjust their behavior to the present situation? The answer is that we are creatures of habit—an overwhelming amount of what we do is automatic. Becoming aware of this got me curious, and as I looked into it a little further, it became a fascination of mine. Since so much of our behavior is determined by habits, my first question is: What is a habit? Dr. Phillippa Lally conducted a groundbreaking study into how habits people form habits. Her definition of a habit is:

> Behaviors which are performed automatically because they have been performed frequently in the past. This repetition creates a mental association between the situation (cue) and action (behavior) which means that when the cue is encountered the behavior is performed automatically. Automaticity has a number of components, one of which is lack of thought.[28]

---

28   Lally, Phillippa, Cornelia H. M. van Jaarsveld, Henry W. W. Potts, and Jane Wardle. 2010. "How Are Habits Formed: Modelling Habit Formation in the Real World." *European Journal of Social Psychology* 40 (6): 998–1009.

When we are operating out of a habit *we* are *not thinking*. How much of your life is performed automatically, without thinking? If you are like me, you will discover that the percentage of habitual behaviors in your everyday life is quite high. I bet you have had the experience of being on your way somewhere and arriving at your destination only to realize that you got there without thinking about the route—your ingrained habits did all of that navigation and negotiating without your being conscious of it.

After reading articles and studies about habitual behavior, my curiosity grew, and I began inquiring into what it takes to break unwanted habits and form ones that are desirable and productive. I began experimenting with simple things, for example the habit of making my bed. Throughout my life, I made my bed sporadically; sometimes I made my bed and sometimes I didn't. This seemed like a good place to start my experiment. I wanted to see if I could commit to something simple like making my bed every single day, thus forming a positive habit where I wouldn't have to think about it.

It was much harder than I thought; especially when I had a lot on my mind, got behind, or was in a hurry. Why? Because my habit was *to make it when I had time and not make it when I was in a rush*. Sound familiar?

I ran across something that made me think of this particular habit, and after listening to it, I decided to do something about it. In a commencement address to the University of Texas at Austin class of 2014, Admiral William H. McRaven shared ten principles to overcome challenges, which he learned while training as a Navy SEAL. Admiral McRaven's speech gave the students ten things that he recommended they do if they wanted to change the world. The first one was: "Make your bed." He explained by doing that as your first act of the day, you start off with an accomplishment and have something that will carry through your day. After reading his speech, I decided that was a good enough reason to make this a habit. However, despite his sound advice, it didn't really help to know that I *should* do it. I found myself restating it and avoiding it, coming up with excuses for not doing it. So, I got intentional about it; in some cases, I had to force myself to do it. Mind you, it only took a few minutes, but I was very aware of my level of resistance to doing it rigorously and consistently. Eventually, it became a natural thing, and I do it now each day without having to think about it. It does makes a difference.

Here is another example of changing an old habit and forming a new one. One day a few years back, I was at the dentist getting my six-month check-up and cleaning from my dentist, Dr. James Granberry, a great guy from Houston with a lovely Texas accent. He came in and had the usual comment: "Your teeth and your gums look great. Are you flossing?" I told him I flossed between five and six times a day.

He said, "I sense some sarcasm," and I copped to the fact that I virtually never floss my teeth.

He responded, "Well, since I know that you know that it is important, I am wondering why you wouldn't do something that is so simple to do."

It was a valid question, so I stopped and thought about it for a moment; I really looked at what it was that kept me from doing something so simple. I told him that I didn't like sticking my fingers in my mouth because it grossed me out.

He asked me if I would be willing to try something that didn't require doing that but would allow me to floss.

I said I would, and he handed me a small packet of thirty floss picks—the little white plastic angled picks, shaped like a tiny wrench with a piece of floss stretched across them.

He asked me to try this for thirty days, and I promised him I would.

I took them home and set them on the bathroom counter next to my toothbrush. Again, there was resistance. Resistance to what? I know it is good for me, I know it only takes a minute to do it, but *I still resisted changing my behavior and breaking the habit of not flossing.* Despite this, I flossed each day for the thirty days until I had used up the initial supply that Jim had given me. Then I did something very wise—I bought more. I kept doing it, and it eventually became a habit; now I do it without thinking. I broke a bad habit and formed a positive one.

You may be saying: "So what? He makes his bed, and he flosses. I've been doing that all my life!" If that is the case, then good for you. The point here is not about an orderly bedroom or oral hygiene—it is about what it takes to break a bad habit and form a habit that supports you. Perhaps for you it is something else, like leaving your workspace organized at the end of the day. Maybe it is managing your calendar, acknowledging birthdays and special occasions, or planning vacations in advance. All of these things are areas where you may have formed habits that you may want to upgrade.

Here is a habit I formed quite a while back: sending handwritten thank you notes to anyone who gives me a gift, whether it be a book or having me over for dinner. I learned this habit years ago from—guess who—my mother. She used to make me get out a stationary pad and write out note when someone did something nice for me. As a result, today I do it religiously and reliably. It is remarkable how people react, particularly nowadays. Invariably, they are both delighted and surprised to receive the note. It is so rare these days to receive anything handwritten in the mail, and sadly in many cases, it is even rare for people to say thank you at all. Recently one of my clients let me know that two of the people that had participated in our Leaders of Our Future course had been promoted to vice presidents. I reached into the left drawer of my desk, in which there is a small supply of assorted occasion cards and envelopes (business ones and blank ones), which I choose depending on the occasion. I took a couple of the business ones with our company logo and spent a few moments writing a note to congratulate both Michael and Brian, who had just been promoted. Within a couple of days and on the same day, both Michael and Brian sent me separate emails and each specifically thanked me for the handwritten note. What more do you need to know about forming that as a habit if you don't already do it? It is a very good practice to have in business especially.

Another practice I have in business is to follow-up every client conversation with an email by (1) recapping the conversation with a set of bullet points for what was covered, (2) listing promises made by me and by them, (3) highlighting the next date we agreed to connect, (4) letting them know that I will send them an invite for that meeting, and (5) asking them to confirm that my recap is on target. This is a habit that will make an enormous difference in your business and your life. Here are some of the benefits:

- ○ You have a full record in writing of what was covered—this eliminates misunderstandings and wrong assumptions.
- ○ You have a record of the promises made. Trust me on this one, as you get older, your memory is not what it used to be.
- ○ You show up organized like a professional and it lends credibility.
- ○ When it is time for the next contact, I pull up the email, review it, and I am fully briefed on the status of the conversation or project, and I am fully prepared for the next call or meeting.

Putting this practice in place has raised my level of professionalism, reliability, and confidence. Making changes in behavior is not easy—it takes focus, determination, and rigor. When you begin to master the technique of converting old negative habits into upgraded positive ones, you will find it easier and easier to accomplish the more challenging ones. Start with something easy and see what happens.

CHAPTER 27

TAKING A STAND

One of the things I really love about my career is the opportunity it affords to work with some truly remarkable leaders. Being around them provides an experience and education that you simply cannot get in business school—it is neither theoretical or hypothetical; it is real time, non-stop, and ever changing.

CEOs are a rare breed of people, particularly the good ones. They know what it means to be responsible and accountable at every level in their company. Exceptional CEOs are willing to own it all and call the shots; they make decisions about the future of the enterprise. They come in all shapes, sizes, colors, education levels, nationalities, and backgrounds. However, the best ones all seem to share two common traits—character and courage. It is their job to invent, design, and strategize a vision for the future. They then articulate that future in such a way that they enroll their people, from the most senior executive team to the newest front-line worker, in that vision. It is a special, unique, and rare ability.

One such person I got to spend time with is a man named Tom Stephens. Tom is quite a character; he has bright red hair and is originally from Arkansas. He's a true Southern gentleman who is smarter than hell and full of charm.

Tom has been the CEO of several companies—Johns Manville, MacMillan Bloedel, and Boise Cascade, to name a few. He has had great success and has earned his reputation. He sits on several boards where he can contribute his vast corporate experience.

A few years back, he was on the board of one such company and its members asked if he would consider running the company. He thought about it long and hard because if he was going to do this, he was going to do it in such a way that it would change the company culture, which would, in turn, reverse the unattractive P&L numbers and correct the company's downward trends. His straightforward approach would involve some big changes, as the culture had become complacent and unproductive. They needed Tom to turn the company around and have it become profitable again. It had four divisions: (1) paper manufacturing, (2) box manufacturing, (3) lumber, and (4) building materials. He agreed to do it.

As is typical, when he took over in the role as CEO, he quickly realized that he was inheriting a situation that was much worse than had been described. This didn't come as a surprise to Tom, as he walked into the role fully expecting it. He also knew that it would probably get worse before it got better. He was prepared to do what needed to be done, and he had a reputation for doing just that.

At the time, I was a partner in a boutique management consulting firm that specialized in transformational work, which is my background. Our firm had a solid relationship with Tom from work on creating a transformation in a forest products company. He had turned that family-owned business around to such an extent that it became attractive enough to be acquired by one of the largest forest products companies in the world. Tom knew how to run a company successfully, how to turn one around, and how to build a culture that was effective and productive. When he entered his new role as CEO, he made it clear to the leadership team that he had certain expectations and no tolerance for mediocrity, equivocating, or justifications. He said there are two kinds of people—people who produce results and people who don't produce results with an excuse. Tom was after the former and had no tolerance for the latter.

The culture in this company was populated by very good people who knew their business. However, it was not very profitable as a result of years of mediocre results and complacency at the top. It had eroded the culture to the point where it had become ordinary, and its leaders were willing to accept sub-par productivity that directly impacted profitability and success. Tom knew he had to infuse new life into this tired company, so he placed focus on four things: (1) safety, (2) productivity, (3) quality, and (4) costs. His ultimate goal was to increase EBITDA (aka, Earnings Before Interest, Taxes, Depreciation, and Amortization).

Tom assembled his key leaders, told them exactly what he wanted from them, and described his approach for transforming the company. He let them know that he was going to bring in the company I was with and use us to help mobilize the front line. He would develop and train everyone, all the way down to frontline employees, by meaningfully engaging them in the business. This had worked for him several times in other companies, resulting in a transformation. He saw that when the employees were given responsibility and were held accountable for the results, they would step up and own the business results.

There was resistance to this approach from the leadership, who had always run the company from a "command-control" style, which essentially translated to giving orders and expecting them to be followed. This old and ineffective style of management produced employees that were there to follow orders and not think as business owners. Consequently, there was a mood of resignation within the ranks that needed to be disrupted and transformed. The mode with the frontline employees had devolved to a "check-your-brain-at-the-door-and-wait-to-be-told-what-to-do" mentality.

Leadership couldn't seem to grasp the context of mobilizing the front line, partially because it was such a foreign concept, partially because it was resisting change, and ultimately because it involved giving up control. Company leaders didn't like what they were hearing, but Tom was not going to acquiesce to their level. Instead, he scheduled a mandatory all-day meeting of everyone in a leadership role, which totaled about fifty-four people from across the four divisions. He asked our company to come in and present the fundamental concepts and vision of what a transformation looks like, why it is required, and how it works.

One of the other partners, Pete Lawrie, and I headed to company headquarters to deliver the presentation and hopefully engage leadership. We had the whole day to do it, and when we arrived we were met some nice, polite, and intelligent people.

However, we could immediately sense their standoffishness, skepticism, and sensed the resistance beneath the surface.

I began laying out the fundamentals of producing a transformation—that we were going to target what Tom referred to as "outrageous results." This was *not* what they were used to. They listened politely, but it was pretty obvious that they were tolerating the presentation and not engaged. We were viewed as "consultants" who knew very little about their company and their industry.

I was three hours into the session and had done a good job of laying it out so they understood the steps and what would be required of them. I felt that they were at least grasping the plan and the approach. Suddenly, Tom got up from his seat at one of the tables about halfway back in the room and headed to the front. He smiled at me and said, "OK that's enough. They have heard enough of what you have to say to get where we are headed."

He stood in the front of the room and said, "Okay, you have a pretty good picture now of where we are going and how we plan to get there. I'm committed to this, and you need to be committed to it as well for this to work. We are taking off on this journey today, so if you're coming along, get on board, and you will be part of something truly amazing. This is my invitation to you, and I want your answer today. For those of you who have reluctance, I am offering a blue-plate special today and today only. If you feel that this is not for you, come and see me in my office today, and I will write you a big fat check with a very attractive severance package that you will find more than generous. In addition, I will write you a glowing letter of recommendation to present to your next employer. Why? Because I want them to hire you. I want you working for our competition. So that's the deal, and it is a one-time deal. Now, if you don't come see me today, that will be your way of letting me know that you are onboard and will fully engage in the transformation that is about to take place here. However, if you don't take the deal today and it becomes clear that you are not onboard—what I call a blocker—you will be asked to leave the company, but without the generous severance package I just spoke about. You will be terminated, and you will be on your own."

The room was silent and still; you could have heard a pin drop. Everyone sat uncomfortably for a moment. Tom then thanked them for coming, told them that he was excited about the future, and was thrilled that they were going to be a part of it. The eight-hour session ended before noon, and they adjourned for lunch. Later in the day, the chief counsel for the company went to see Tom and submitted his resignation. He was at that point in his career that it was only a matter of time and thought it was good timing, particularly with the generous severance package that was being offered.

The company did, in fact, produce a transformation in several of their divisions and profitability began to increase. It was slow at first, but as the employees became more and more empowered, they began producing truly remarkable results in all four areas. Safety accidents decreased dramatically, production run rates began breaking company records, quality went up considerably, and the company's costs were contained. What was remarkable about this transformation was that the frontline employees were clearly producing these results, and it was obvious that a shift had taken place.

Tom Stephens took a stand for transforming the company— he did it with a lot of resistance, but he never wavered, nor did he capitulate. He stood for "outrageous results," empowering his people, and it paid off in spades.

Later, I had a chance to meet with Tom to discuss progress on the transformation project. I was proud of what we had accomplished together and was in awe of his leadership. I took the opportunity to ask him a question about what he saw as the key to producing a successful transformation. He had a very interesting reply. "Most CEOs don't realize what their job really is—many of them think they are supposed to run the company and know everything about it. They couldn't be more mistaken, and if they are focused on those things, they will certainly fail as the chief executive officer. A CEO has three main responsibilities:

1. To put together a talented and reliable team of leaders—people who can and will successfully run their business unit. If the CEO is running the day-to-day business, they have the wrong person in whatever part of the business they are running or getting involved in. They have to get the right people in the right roles, trust them to make the right decisions and hold them accountable for those decisions.

2. A CEO should be focused on the long-term future, economic trends, changes in the market, and customer demand for their products, now and in the future. In short, they need to have a good idea of what the next five years is likely to look like, how they can improve the outlook of what is predictable and position the company for future success. Therefore, the CEO's job is not to have all of the answers—instead, they need to be asking the right questions.

3. They have to have a vision that they believe in, which will appeal to and become infectious to employees. With that firm belief, they will have a positive story to tell the investors. This will drive confidence and boost their stock price and the company's value.

Very rarely do you find a wise and brilliant leader like Tom Stephens. Throughout my career, I have had the good fortune to work with several truly extraordinary leaders who know the power of taking a stand.

CHAPTER 28

BEING INCLUSIVE

We have become very polarized. Our nation has become separated through divergent conversations, dialogues, and opinions more than ever before. It seems to have been heading in that direction for some time, and the emergent participation in social media and less traditional news outlets have raised the volume on and exacerbated our differences. It's actually gone beyond having different points of view; we have begun to dislike and isolate ourselves from those who disagree with us. We've become so divided that we've lost our ability to discuss, debate, and argue in a dignified way. It seems that we can no longer have differing points of view without our discussions quickly spiraling into personal attacks. I call this phenomenon the "either/or" syndrome. This means it's either my way (which is right), or it's your way (which is wrong), and there's no room for any other viewpoint. We no longer look to find common ground or try to understand the reasoning behind the other view and whether or not it has value for consideration. We have become unsophisticated, awkward, mean, and sometimes vulgar with one another when we have disagreements or opposing views.

Disagreement and debate are at the foundation of our culture. It's what has allowed this country to grow and thrive for centuries. Yet that very underpinning is quickly disintegrating right before our eyes. Former President Bill Clinton shared a snippet from a book in which he pointed to this dilemma for us as a nation. He said:

> I read a book a couple of years ago that I recommend to people all the time called *The Big Sort* by Bill Bishop who is a journalist and as it happens a pretty progressive Democrat from Austin, Texas. And what provoked him to write this book was his neighborhood in Austin lost its only Republican neighbor. And he loved this guy. And he talked about how their kids played together, and they took walks together. And how much he learned from their arguments because they didn't see everything the same way and how much it meant to him to know there was somebody he liked and respected and cared for that he could actually have an honest discussion where neither one of them would be completely predictable. But, he said, I was the only one of our neighbors who was nice to him. Now, in their neighborhood in the 2004 presidential election Senator Kerry defeated President Bush three to

one. So, the Republican guy moves out and moves into another neighborhood in Austin, Texas where President Bush defeated Senator Kerry four to one. And Bishop said, you know both of our neighborhoods were poorer for that. He pointed out that in 1976 when Jimmy Carter and Gerald Ford had a razor thin election, which by the way, ultimately culminated in a lifetime friendship between the two of them until President Ford passed away. But anyway, in that election—a one percent election—only twenty percent of America's counties voted for one or the other of them by twenty percent or more. Which meant that in 1976, you could go into any coffee shop or hair salon or barber shop or bowling alley and have a conversation with people who didn't necessarily disagree with you about what was going on in America. By 2004, when President Bush won the closest re-election margin of any reelected President since Woodrow Wilson in 1916, forty-eight percent of our counties voted for one or the other of them by more than twenty percent. That much movement. So, he said you know America's making real progress, this Bishop guy said, we're not as racist as we used to be, we're not as sexist as we used to be, we're not as homophobic as we used to be. *The only bigotry we have left is that we just don't want to be around anyone who disagrees with us.*[29]

---

29   *President Bill Clinton on Political Disagreement.* 2012b. US: YouTube. https://youtu.be/5rjOSfYc5yA.

My guess is that you've experienced what Clinton is referring to. We don't discuss anymore; we speak and don't listen. In doing this, we miss the opportunity to discover our amazing ability to come to an agreement that's workable for everyone. It's as though we've regressed to a child's approach of "if I don't get my way, then I gotta make sure you don't get yours."

Everyone is familiar with the biblical story of King Solomon and the two women who had a baby and couldn't decide to whom the baby belonged. The king, in frustration, offered his solution and told them they would just split the baby in half and share it. It was his way of showing them the absurdity of their inability to come to some acceptable solution. It seems that we are unwilling to consider any alternative other than "I'm right."

The solution to this problem is to be able to have a conversation in which we consider the other person's point of view as valid. It is not right or wrong; in fact, another's view is just as valid as our point of view. From there, we can begin to have a dialogue that is focused on what's possible as the end result.

Right now, our elected officials sit at a cool 15 percent approval rating, primarily because they don't seem to get anything done.[30] This can be attributed to the fact that they disagree and won't have the tough discussions that are needed to get to a place where they can agree. So, the conversation shuts down, and just like children, they take their marbles and go home. We can't let it be resolved as Clinton said about Bill Bishop, the author of *The Big Sort, "The only bigotry we have left is that we just don't want to be around anyone who disagrees with us."* It must start with each of us taking a stand to transform the conversation and return to civility.

---

30   "U.S. Congress - Public Approval Rating 2021." n.d. Statista.Com. Accessed June 28, 2021. https://www.statista.com/statistics/207579/public-approval-rating-of-the-us-congress/.

CHAPTER 29

THE FREE
FISH METHOD

When you work in an organization, you become aware that there's a lot of "politics" involved. If you're going to succeed, you can't ignore it because it's part of the fabric. Small things can become big things, and people can often be very petty. There are a lot of gossips in organizations, and one of the things I've learned over the years is that gossip is one of the most destructive things that exists. Part of our consulting practice involves teaching people how to listen effectively and speak straight with one another—that is, to get things on the table in such a way that they get resolved and don't persist as an issue.

Frequently, we're asked to come in and work on what I call "squabbles," where two highly paid professionals are not seeing eye to eye on one or several things. They tend to get into these dead-end conversations and are essentially at loggerheads. Things slow down or stop as a result.

One of the keys to being an effective executive is knowing which battles are worth fighting and which ones are not. Most people are familiar with the "80/20" rule, where 80 percent of your value or profit comes from 20 percent of your customers. The 80/20 principle can be mapped onto many situations, but one of the most interesting ways to look at it is in organizations. I've asked hundreds of executives: "If 20 percent of your people are your top performers and they deliver 80 percent of the positive results and value that your organization delivers, then would it make good sense to spend most of your time working with those people?"

Most executives tell me that they end up spending most of their time with the low performers, dealing with the issues, problems, and squabbles that they seem to dwell on. We try to get them to focus on the things that make a difference and not get sucked into irrelevant matters.

One of my clients is absolutely brilliant at navigating this very thing—her name is Elizabeth Killinger. I've been working with her since 2002, so we have a long history of producing some pretty amazing things. Elizabeth is one of the best people I have ever seen at navigating the politics of an organization. In the time I've known her, she's worked for several different people and reported directly to a number of different CEOs or COOs, each of them with very different personalities, approaches, and managing styles. Somehow, Elizabeth is able to connect, align, and work with them in true partnership. I credit this with her ability to recognize what matters to her boss, work with that person's particular style, and deliver stunning results, which she has done throughout her career. I've often told her that she has a real gift in this area, and Elizabeth, being quite humble, accepts the compliments.

I once asked her what made her so successful at it. She said, "I focus on the big items and don't get hung up on the little things. There are battles worth fighting, and there are battles not worth fighting. You definitely want to know which to fight and I select mine very carefully. I don't want to win all the battles; I want to win the battles that matter."

Here's an example of a time where I witnessed her prowess at this. She was running the retail division of a large energy company. She and her leadership team had decided that they wanted to bring our firm in to do some development of the next level of people, which they referred to as "high po's." These are people that show high potential for the future, and she wanted to give them as much leadership development and training as possible to give them the best advantage in moving up in their careers.

Elizabeth and her leadership team asked me to come in and what I was thinking for a good-sized group of targeted directors and managers. I prepared a presentation, and they scheduled me to present it to her and her eight direct reports, many of whom had been through a similar training.

On the day of the presentation, they were already in the meeting room and when it was time for me to start, they called me in. I was taken aback for a moment—Elizabeth was at the head of a boardroom-style table flanked by her direct reports, all of whom were men, all about the same age (in their forties), and in what looked like corporate uniforms; they all had clean-cut haircuts and button-down, collared shirts. I knew most of these people, but I hadn't seen them together before. I smiled, and she asked why. I said, "These guys all look the same." She responded, "These are my guys." (And to their credit, each one of them is a really great person whom I've gotten to know over the years.)

I began laying out the program that I had developed, which we called "Being a Great Leader." It included being a better communicator, delegating effectively, managing teams, and a host of other topics. I assumed that they wanted to offer the program with a mix of managers and directors in each of the courses. They questioned this assumption because they felt that the directors should be in one group and the managers should be in a different group. So, there were two options on the table—my firm could provide the training to a combination of managers and directors, or we could separate the directors from the managers so that the directors received one level of training (slightly more advanced), while the managers would participate in a more basic program.

Virtually all of the people in the room, except Elizabeth, thought the two groups should be isolated and trained separately, keeping their titles distinct. She disagreed, saying, "Separating them will make no difference. They should all receive the same training, and it will work just fine." Elizabeth viewed it as an opportunity for them to interact and relate, which she considered a positive. However, the leadership team did not come to a decision at that meeting; they were at a stalemate. I agreed to see if I could get it resolved within the week by having conversations with the individual stakeholders. Almost all of the key leaders who were in the room held the position that the two trainings should be kept separate. When I went back to Elizabeth and told her that they felt pretty strongly about it, she smiled and said, "Then let them have it; they get to win this one. They're wrong, but I'm not taking that one on."

I was surprised by her response because I knew she felt firmly about her thinking. I asked, "Just like that, huh?"

She said, "Look, we get into these 'little battles' pretty regularly. This one isn't worth fighting. Sometimes it's best to let them win in a scuffle like this because it ultimately makes no difference. I choose my battles wisely and when I need to win the battle, I want to make sure it's one worth fighting for. This one is not worth it, so I'll consider it a *free fish*.[31] And it costs me nothing. Ultimately, the point is to get everyone trained, which will happen either way."

They wanted to win the debate, and Elizabeth let them. This demonstrated to me that she was using her wisdom to determine where she was going to invest her time and energy. As leaders, we are required to invest our time in a great many undertakings, much of which isn't leading. I have seen the free fish technique work brilliantly with teams in negotiations and even at home. Try it out and see how it works for you.

---

31   The reference about a free fish comes from the training of dolphins. They are very smart mammals, probably the most intelligent next to humans. They learn very quickly because they are rewarded with a fish when they do tricks. Every so often, for no reason at all, dolphin trainers throw the dolphin a fish. The dolphins know that and pay close attention to the trainer at all times in the hopes they might get a spontaneous free fish.

CHAPTER 30

THINK CLEARLY TO WRITE CLEARLY

Wisdom from Elizabeth Neeld

Years ago, I became aware of the importance of writing in my career as a consultant. It is not sufficient to merely be a good management consultant, you must be able to articulate ideas effectively and clearly. This is easier said than done. When you ask the client to consider a different approach, quite often, they are married to how they think or embedded in how things have been done before. The challenge is to describe the situation and paint a picture of the future in such a way that it becomes possible and real for them.

Years ago, in my previous firm, we became aware of how important writing was and soon discovered that our writing skills were not at the level they should be for a professional management consultancy, so we decided to contract the services of a formidable writing coach, Elizabeth Harper Neeld. Elizabeth has had several careers; she's been an English professor at Texas A&M University, an executive for Shell Oil, a management consultant and is now a passionate writer and writing coach. She has written twenty-six books and was selected by Nightingale-Conant to produce an audio series called *Yes! You Can Write.*

Elizabeth came to our firm to teach writing to all of the consultants. I found her class very engaging and soaked in everything she said. From this, I requested that she work with me as a writing coach, which she did for the next two years.

Elizabeth made a very clear statement as she began that first session: "You don't have a writing problem; you have a thinking problem."

She continued by pointing out that anyone can just start writing but writing something that people will want to read, that they will follow and understand, and that will make a positive difference, was an art.

Elizabeth taught me how to think so I could write effectively, vividly, and clearly. She introduced the idea of creating a blueprint, which I would do before writing a single word. It served to develop my thinking and order it in a clear and cohesive manner that would follow a theme while delivering key ideas through the use of examples in order to deliver a cogent message for the reader. Almost immediately, my productivity and my success rate went up because I was articulating concepts and paradigms clearly and accurately for my clients.

If you have ever tried to write, you probably know that it is a bit like singing in the shower—you may think that you're able to duplicate the voice of Don Henley of the Eagles, and you just might have missed your calling. However, if you listen to your voice on a recording, you will quickly hear that you do not sound anything like the Don Henley, and an impartial listener will probably think your voice is awful. Writing is similar—as you write, it may seem like a flow of divine inspiration brought forth by an avatar. Yet when you read it out loud, it is not quite how you imagined it—in fact, it is disjointed, rambling, and fails to hit the intended mark. Effective writing requires you to think about how the reader is going to read the piece—does it logically follow a thought pattern? Does one idea build on the previous one and so forth?

What I confirmed was exactly what I had previously learned in the class that Elizabeth taught me, which is if you outline your writing piece in advance, clearly in order, you will find that you're able to write something that is clear, easy to follow, and digest.

CHAPTER 31

HIGH-PERFORMANCE TEAMS

Seventy percent of all strategic program initiatives fail. Our firm has discovered that much of the problem occurs in the way people work together, communicate with each other, and support one another. The level of integrity that's present among the team and in the project, as well as the way in which they each regard one another, will determine whether the initiative succeeds. Our firm has developed five essential practices for building high-performance teams:

1. Authentic Listening

   This is easier said than done as most people think they are good listeners, but this is simply not true. Authentic listening requires the ability to get in another's world, not just their words, but the place from which they are speaking and understanding what they intend to say. Two good habits to develop this skill are giving the speaker your undivided attention and repeating what you heard back to the person with what you think is his or her intention. This gives the speaker an opportunity to confirm or correct your feedback.

2. Talking Straight

This means putting things on the table that are difficult or uncomfortable to address in such a way that everyone is left feeling respected, honored, and empowered. At the same time, it's essential to get the elephant in the room dealt with head on. There is a fine line between confronting something that is difficult to talk about and doing so with the sensitivity it requires. This takes courage and grace at the same time.

3. Working as a Team

Watch any professional sports team, and the teamwork is apparent. Teamwork requires a "pit crew" mentality. Each person backs up, supports, and empowers the others, and their win belongs to each of them. Team members say, "Your win is my win. Your loss is my loss." They work together in such a way that extraordinary results take place. No one gets toppled by little things, and nothing gets in the way.

4. Honoring Your Word

If this doesn't happen, you can forget the rest. This is simply working towards doing what you say you will do. It's doing what you know to do, what's expected, and what you know is right. Everybody knows how to do this, but do they do it? Fundamental to this strategy is acknowledging mistakes and cleaning up any messes from not delivering on promises. When you make a mess, the best way to handle it is to clean it up immediately and move on. Cleanup on aisle four!

5. Being Complete

Being complete means that you don't step over trash. If something needs to be said, dealt with, or cleared up, you do so right away. The people on your team collectively understand that when they operate without dealing with negative issues, resentments, or things unsaid, everything comes to a grinding halt. The point is to get things dealt with completely so there is no residue. In doing so, the team cultivates an appreciation for the practice of keeping things "clean." In sports, you can see the guys in the dugout or on the court high-fiving each other when each little win happens throughout the game. This is no different than validating success in business.

By having these five practices in place, you can build a high-performance team. We've seen that when teams have these five components working actively, the likelihood of success turns around dramatically, from a 70 percent likelihood of failure to an 85 percent likelihood of success, which we have demonstrated in our work with clients over the years.

Portions of the material in this chapter are derived from the work of Werner Erhard and Landmark Worldwide, LLC and are used with permission.

CHAPTER 32

THE RIGHT PEOPLE—A TRIM TAB

Wisdom from Regina Mellinger

The "Trim Tab Effect" was used by the late Buckminster Fuller, an American philosopher, systems theorist, architect, and inventor. I met him years ago, and his explanation of it has impacted me ever since. This theory describes the possibility of making something happen more efficiently without exerting more effort. Bucky said:

> Think of the Queen Mary—the whole ship goes by and then comes the rudder. And there's a tiny thing on the edge of the rudder called a trim tab. It's a miniature rudder. Just moving that little trim-tab builds a low pressure that pulls the rudder around...Takes almost no effort at all.... But if you're doing dynamic things mentally, the fact is

that you can just put your foot out like that and the whole big ship of state is going to go. So, I said, Call me Trim Tab."[32]

Consider your hiring process. You're not going to be happy if you hire the wrong person. Anyone who has done so knows exactly what we're talking about. It takes a lot of time to recognize that you've hired the wrong person, and it takes more time to admit it to yourself, to adjust to it, and to attempt to fix the problem. After all that, it takes yet more time to fire that person. Then you have to start the process over again, using up more time, more energy, and more money.

Instead, why not have a process that makes something happen more efficiently without exerting more effort. *Trim Tab.* Here's the process we designed to ensure a good hire:

1. *Start with good, qualified candidates.* We hire a good placement firm for this.
   - The candidates are pre-screened for their skill level. For example, in our firm, it is essential that the right hire is competent in all Microsoft processes.
   - The placement firm will pre-test and pre-qualify candidates before referring them.
   - The firm will also conduct a thorough background check. (Don't underestimate the value of this. I have, and it has backfired on us.) *Trim Tab.*

---

32 "A Quote by R. Buckminster Fuller." n.d. Goodreads.Com. Accessed June 28, 2021. https://www.goodreads.com/quotes/2388932-something-hit-me-very-hard-once-thinking-about-what-one.

2. *Conduct a thorough interview process.* There should be more than one interview with several people interviewing each potential hire. Sometimes, there is the right chemistry with one person, but another manager may not have the same experience. We conduct three interviews: the initial interview, the call back, and a final interview. Simultaneously, we interview several other candidates, rather than having a linear process. This will expedite things significantly. *Trim Tab.*

3. *Test their skill.* Give the potential candidates a task to complete. It is essential that our employees are facile with generating PowerPoint presentations, as we do a lot of these with clients. Usually, the assigned task is to provide a fourteen-page presentation to "tell us why we should hire you." The document should represent who you are and what you are about. The purpose of this is to present yourself as the best person for the job. This will give us a chance to find out more about you and show us the quality of the work you do, how you think of yourself, how you think and approach a situation, and how you think you might fit in with Leadera, our company. We then give examples slide by slide of how the person might complete the task and provide simple, clear directions such as, "Complete the following assignment and send it back within twenty-four hours." Following directions is a *must.* I've learned a lot from this step as well; how a person follows directions is essential to the fulfilling success of the firm. *Trim Tab.*

4. *Trust your instinct.* Recognize the difference between what's on paper versus what your gut is telling you. Some candidates may have all the right qualifications, but sometimes, something about them tells you they are not quite right. Determine the difference between their credibility versus how they "show up" for you in person. *Trim Tab.*

5. *Bring them into a public setting.* We want to know what it's going to be like working with this person and how they behave in real life. We take the candidate out for a lunch or dinner meeting. There, we can see how he or she interacts with people, which can be more revealing than an interview. How does the person treat the waitstaff? How does he place an order, off the menu or by special request? Is the person easy to interact with socially? Where is his attention focused—on himself or others? *Trim Tab.*

CHAPTER 33

STAYING THE COURSE

As we already discussed, 70 percent of strategic initiatives in companies fail. Research points to four key contributing factors. The first is that people in the company don't really know the employer's vision and are not aligned with where the company needs to go. Second, they don't know their specific role in delivering on what the company is trying to accomplish. Third, they don't have a clear, transparent scorecard that is in use, kept up-to-date, accurate or complete. Fourth, people are not being held accountable.

In studying project management effectiveness, we have found that when these four components are solidly in place, the likelihood of success goes up dramatically. More importantly, with initiatives that fail, we've discovered that they didn't build these four components into the design of the plan.

Additionally, we often find that project teams start with a plan but don't stay committed to it. Worse yet, if the project goes off course even slightly, they sometimes abandon the strategy because they don't trust the thought process that went into it. This is a fatal error and a rookie mistake. Teams have to believe in their plan.

Sticking to the plan takes courage and discipline. It's human nature to doubt and to want to change the program when something unexpected comes along, which almost always happens. We have a strong need for immediate gratification—we want to see instant success and not getting it triggers uncertainty and doubt, so we question the method. Successful project execution requires managers and teams to trust the plan and follow the steps. That means taking the next step, and the next step, and the next step after that.

That is not to say that there isn't room to make changes or adjustments. In fact, the plan may need to change several times. General Dwight D. Eisenhower said, "Only a fool goes into battle without a plan. But only an idiot follows the plan once the battle begins."[33] While you have to be able to make the right adjustments, they should be made while not changing the overall course of your original approach.

Nick Saban, head football coach at the University of Alabama, calls his plans on the field "The Process." It is the blueprint to winning and the way winning is accomplished. Sometimes you start

---

33   Ratcliffe, Susan. 2016. *Oxford Essential Quotations*. 4th ed. London, England: Oxford University Press.

executing the strategy, something happens, and suddenly people abandon it. People stop trusting the plan; they have a tangible reaction to what they're seeing in front of them. Saban's success can be attributed to staying the course and trusting the process. It almost doesn't matter what you see at the line of scrimmage. He tells his players, "Ignore the scoreboard. Don't worry about winning. Just focus on doing your job at the highest level every single play and the wins will follow."[34] Saban shows his players exactly how to execute the move. He never sells out.

When you believe in setting the right values and have faith in your strategy, one of the hardest things to do is to stick with it in the face of circumstances that are not what you want or expect. Staying the course when the going gets tough takes courage.

That 70 percent of failed initiatives are a function of abandoning the plan. The value is in sticking to the plan. Believe in yourself. Trust in the plan. Know in your gut that the plan is correct and see it through to fulfillment. A culture of mistrust develops in organizations that give up on plans and change strategy midstream. When this happens, people become disempowered. They start to think that management is presenting the "flavor of the month" and think "this too shall pass." As a result, employees start second-guessing themselves and quit executing the original design and plans. People sell out easily in that scenario.

There is enormous value in sticking with the plan. Focus on staying the course, which lead to wins for both employees and their employers.

---

34   "A Quote by R. Buckminster Fuller." n.d. Goodreads.Com. Accessed June 28, 2021. https://www.goodreads.com/quotes/2388932-something-hit-me-very-hard-once-thinking-about-what-one.

CHAPTER 34

JOB NUMBER TWO
FOR A LEADER

M ost leaders got into their position by being competent managers, who things happen, solve problems, and get the trains to run on time. However, simply managing the present is insufficient when you become a leader. A leader's job is to focus on the future and create a vision that inspires their people to make it happen.

The main job of a leader is to have a vision that is compelling, inspiring, and achievable and share that vision with their employee's in such a way that see that they not only want to be a part of it, but will also own it so that it comes to fruition. People want to make a difference. They want to have their lives matter. George Bernard Shaw said, "This is the true joy in life, the being used for a purpose recognized by yourself as a mighty one; the being thoroughly worn out before you are thrown on the scrap heap; the being a force of Nature instead of a feverish selfish little clod of ailments and grievances complaining that the world will not devote itself to making you happy."[35]

Creating a vision to engage others with is tricky because it needs to be articulated in such a way that people can hear it, identify with it, and want to participate in it. There are many examples of this in the last decade. Apple's Steve Jobs declared there would be "an Apple on every desk." Jeff Bezos' original mantra was "get big fast." Elon Musk is known for his vision of getting "anywhere on Earth in under one hour." Each of these executives have demonstrated the importance of this vital aspect of leadership by stepping out into the future, creating a vision for what's possible in their company, and going after it with an unrivaled ferocity. Part of this brilliance has to do with the way they are able to present their vision to employees so that they know it's doable. By doing this, a leader ensures that their employees become a part of implementing the vision. Getting people to buy into your vision gives you a huge advantage for success.

Leaders walk people through the vision—what it will take, how it will unfold, and underline the benefits and rewards. At Leadera Consulting, we have a nine-point, step-by-step formula in which we train leaders on how to deliver a powerful leadership message focusing on the future. When they design a message using these points in this specific order, they find that their employees are able to connect with their vision, have it become tangible, and want to participate in delivering it. The nines points are:

---

35   Shaw, George Bernard. n.d. "Thoughts On The Business of Life." Forbes. com. Accessed June 27, 2021.

1. Background connection
2. The vision
3. Strategy
4. Implications
5. Actions needed
6. Sense of urgency
7. Benefits and rewards
8. Hardball issues
9. Appreciation and acknowledgement

It is important that the message be delivered in this order. We have found that it is consistent with the way people think. If you're interested in our process, please visit "The Power of Your Leadership Message" on our website, Leaderacg.com.

Successful leaders love to inspire their people. Getting your staff to buy into your message is what allows it to be fulfilled. When done effectively, inspiration leads others into action.

However, keep in mind that the message and that inspiration has no shelf life on its own. A successful leader will build regular and consistent reminders in the workplace that reinforce the message. Inspiration must be shored up with actions. Consider designing how to get your employees on board and how to keep them there.

CHAPTER 35

THE POWER OF ENROLLMENT

A nyone who occupies a leadership role wants to be an effective leader. We want to take actions that are meaningful, inspire others to action, and fulfill a vision for the future. That's our job.

However, direct action doesn't happen automatically or instantly without some pre-planning. To move a team, a company, or even a person, the leader has to establish a relationship with that person or group in which their constituents belong. More than ever, and especially today, giving orders does not work, except in the rare circumstances that we'll address later. We have found that what is most effective in developing a background of relatedness is having a relationship with a person or group that fosters affinity, respect, admiration, and connection. It is a leader's job to establish this background of relatedness.

A background of relatedness is the first step in moving something to action in a process we call "enrollment." It begins with establishing a relationship in which two parties discover mutually shared goals or commitments. This can be anything from having children who attend the same school to working together on a research and development project in a biotech company.

Imagine that you arrive at an airport. You go outside to get a taxi. And as you're waiting, you're next to someone who is also waiting for a taxi. You both begin to chit chat, and you soon discover that there are no taxis. You ask the other person, "Where are you going?"

"Midtown," they say.

"Oh, I'm going to midtown too, would you like to share a cab?"

Of course, they agree, and when the first taxi finally pulls up, you both get in.

That collaborative action began as casual banter. That friendly exchange set the stage for discovering that you were both going to the same place. You both had the same goal and predicament and discovered how you could solve the problem by solving it together. This simple example illustrates how a background of relatedness works.

One of the challenges a leader has is getting employees on board or getting them to buy into a vision and execute the strategy. How to best articulate their vision is a common challenge for most leaders. What do you say? How do you say it? And what medium is most effective to reach your employees? I have asked more than 10,000 professionals what they consider the worst method for communication, and the unanimous response is through email! Yet I still see many leaders trying to get their people to implement difficult and complex strategies by sending out emails with instructions. *This never ever works!* Fundamentally, people don't like being told what to do, and they resist it. One exception is in the military where the rules of the game are very different, as is the background of relatedness. Yet, you would be surprised at how often people try to do this. Getting people on board requires a bit of a courtship, you need to cultivate the conversation so that they see the sense of it and the value of what it is you're going to ask them to do.

When a leader is initiating a new project, the first step is gathering a key group of people and explaining the necessary steps toward fulfillment. For this to be successful, that conversation must be grounded in a strong background of relatedness. Before asking for anything, a thoughtful leader starts by recognizing and appreciating several things about their team. The leader might begin by thanking people for coming to the meeting, recognizing their recent hard work and validating of highlighting recent wins.

It may go like this: "Good morning everybody. Thank you for being here. I know we're busy trying to get the third quarter results in, and I appreciate how hard everybody has been working. To be clear, it's paying off with some exceptional results, particularly this quarter. I can't thank you enough."

Once the stage is set by establishing a background of relatedness, you can then introduce what's next, including asking people to get on board for the next phase of work or strategic initiative. At that point, you can initiate a sense of urgency, but not until you have established that by listening to your staff. This background of relatedness is the key ingredient in a set of conversations that lead to breakthrough results.

Portions of the material in this chapter are derived from the work of Werner Erhard and Landmark Worldwide LLC and are used with permission.

CHAPTER 36

INVESTING IN
YOUR PEOPLE

aking time to develop yourself and your employees is the best investment you can make, bar none. Your staff is the heart and soul of your organization, and when they develop, you and your organization advance, your product and services improve, and profitability goes up. Investing in their development is a no brainer.

As a leader, you inspire and enable your employees to work toward a common goal and align with the vision for your company. (Hopefully, you will be using some of the strategies that I have outlined throughout this book.) However, training and developing employees at different levels of your company requires a conscious effort and approach. That's why you should consider using a coach for yourself and everyone in your company.

Working with a coach opens up possibilities that wouldn't appear if you were training employees on your own. You often see something that you couldn't see before, and this new awareness can lead you to be more effective and productive. A coach guides you in the areas you can't see or figure out for yourself.

Perhaps you've tried to teach yourself to play an instrument, get your finances in order, or get yourself in shape, but you can only go so far on your own. When you hire a coach, you have someone who has the skills and expertise to help you further develop the proficiencies you need to perform well. Having a structure or program is a worthwhile investment. Your progress will become smoother, go faster, and be accomplished less painfully.

A good example of this is Aaron Judge of the New York Yankees. Judge is one of the most exciting baseball players on the scene today. Even in his rookie year, observers said that he may become one of the greatest players ever; he already has a great hitting average and has made several home run records.

When Aaron he was interviewed about how he became so effective, he said that the previous season his batting average was 179. He wrote down that number and kept it on display on his phone to remind himself to work harder each day. He also immersed himself in a specific structure with a coach. Today his batting average is 329. His successful performance is directly connected with hard work, good coaching, and determination.

When you invest in your people, you commit to their successes. If you were going to build a house, you'd hire an experienced contractor. You wouldn't do it yourself. When you are developing your employees, you should take the same approach. Whether you are introducing a new technology into your organization or learning the latest techniques and strategies, hire an expert to teach your staff from the very beginning. This will ensure that your employees take the new training seriously, while simultaneously committing to long-lasting results. The trainer you hire has the knowledge, skills, and experience to train accurately and efficiently.

Companies sometimes opt to contain costs by postponing the use of outside trainers and coaches for employee training and development; managers often want to see whether an employee has proven him or herself to decide whether to invest more. However, this postponement often backfires, particularly with millennials, who have a desire and need for development. If the opportunity to grow and develop is not present at a company, there is usually a higher rate of attrition. Studies have shown that 40 percent of undertrained employees will leave their positions before the first year is over because of the lack of training and development opportunities. Well-trained employees are more likely to be productive, experience greater job satisfaction, and, therefore, grow with the organization. Though training and developing new employees requires a financial investment, having to go through the process of recruiting and rehiring can be far more expensive. Training and developing your employees are the best investments you can make in your organization.

CHAPTER 37

MAKING PROJECTS SUCCEED

There's a plaque in my office that was given to me in appreciation of some work I did for a client's company that reads: "In appreciation of your contribution to creating 1.5 billion dollars in added value to our company." It represents some work I did for a client on an eighteen-month project that was successfully delivered on time, above what was promised, and without a negative impact on the day-to-day. In my business we call that a *breakthrough.*

I have received several such plaques, certificates, and trophies from clients over the years, and they are nicely displayed atop bookcases scattered around my office in Houston. They have become part of the background, so I don't really notice them, but when I do notice them, I recall how much hard work went into the accomplishments that they represent and how much fun it was to receive them. Maybe a year or longer of dedicated work is summed up in a few words on a plaque signifying a victory for their company, division, or team, and I have learned to derive my satisfaction and fulfillment from these large-scale projects versus "quick fixes," which give immediate gratification but don't really alter the culture or the mindset.

Companies hire our firm because when we assist, they are able to conquer the toughest part of executing a strategy—implementation. That's where strategies usually fail, and they fail more than they succeed. The Project Management Institute (PMI) reports that 72 percent of corporate projects fail or fall short.[36] This means that they do not deliver the promised results; they don't deliver the results on time; they don't come in on budget; and they don't deliver the value they had promised. These failures deteriorate confidence within the organization, which leads to doubt and suspicion. The lack of trust makes future promises highly questionable and unreliable, weighing on morale.

When people hear of the 72 percent failure rate, they find it hard to believe because the percentage is so high. Nevertheless, in my experience, this occurs in hundreds of companies, large and small. The way one executive described it to me was, "We have lots of takeoffs with very few landings."

Why is that, you ask?

The answer is fairly simple, and it is explained brilliantly in a book by Chris McChesney, Sean Covey, and Jim Huling called *The 4 Disciplines of Execution.* The authors had conducted a study of over 100,000 strategic initiatives that had been launched in various companies around the world with the predictable 72 percent

---

36   PMBOK® Guide (2021).

rate of failure or falling short. They discovered that there were four common characteristics missing in the projects that failed:

1. People are not clear about where the company wants to go.
2. People are not clear what their role is in delivering success.
3. They do not have an effective scorecard.
4. People are not held accountable.

Conversely, when they looked at the projects that were successful and delivered on time and on budget as promised, they reported that these same four characteristics were fully present and visible:

1. Clear on the vision and values—people in the company were overwhelmingly aware of and knowledgeable about where the company wanted to go.
2. Clear expectations—people understood and knew what their role was in delivering success.
3. A clear and transparent scorecard was in place that gave feedback on employee progress.
4. A reliable reporting structure was in place—people were held to account.

A solid structure sends a positive message and ensures engagement at a certain level. However, just putting these four structures in isn't enough; leaders must also send a positive message throughout the organization.

Additionally, the vision and strategy must be real to people. Think of it like this—until the receptionist knows the strategy, you don't really have a strategy. This requires a campaign of communication. Mobilizing the workforce is highly underestimated, yet essential.

CHAPTER 38

CULTURE DRIVES BEHAVIOR

Step back and look at any organization—what you will see is the manifestation of its culture. People inside the company operate consistently with whatever culture has been established or set. By culture, I mean the values, themes, behaviors, passions, expressions, and actions that take place inside a group—in this case, a company. Culture gets established by a combination of:

- how the company was built,
- its history and evolution, and
- the leadership being provided.

The leader's job is to create a culture that serves the needs of the stakeholders and people inside and outside the company, meaning employees, customers, and suppliers. Whether or not the culture's characteristics are openly clear to the people in the organization will dictate the extent to which the people themselves operate consistently with the culture.

Obviously, it's most effective when those values and behaviors are made public and visible to everyone in the organization. We have found that the best way to do this is to have those values in writing, or talked about regularly. Several of our clients have done a splendid job of doing this and, in one company in particular, it's pretty hard to walk down a hallway and not see its values posted for all to see.

In our experience, the companies that do this well have employees who are keenly aware of these values and are more likely to operate consistently with them when they are vividly displayed.

There are some recent examples of well-known companies that went off course because their values were not sufficiently clear to the management and employees. One such example is Wells Fargo Bank, an institution that built its reputation on integrity, trust, and financial prudence, which translates to "you can trust our company with your money."

However, at some point, people in the company began managing growth and new customer acquisitions at any cost. They incentivized gaining new customer accounts over being trusted custodians of their customers' finances. The compensation system began to reward people making the numbers versus people providing excellent service and solid financial guidance. Consequently, Wells Fargo employees began inventing fraudulent new accounts using established customers' data without their awareness or permission. This unethical behavior was inconsistent with what Wells

Fargo has stood for since the bank was founded more than a century ago. How could this possibly happen?

It happened because integrity got replaced by greed. The culture had become corrupted. The leadership began striving for near-term gains and abandoned the timeless values that made the company successful for decades.

When all of this was discovered and publicized, Wells Fargo lost the confidence and trust of the public. The company is now hard at work trying to rebuild that trust and reformulate a culture that was seemingly destroyed in a relatively short period of time. Wells Fargo has invested millions of dollars to market contrite apologies and is begging for another chance to prove its values to customers.

Another example of a corporate culture going off course is Facebook. Facebook made its mark through its original design to serve people by connecting them and providing a platform where they could share their most personal details, family events, and special occasions, while also connecting with old friends and lost relatives. It fulfilled that purpose for many years, delivering unimaginable growth for well over a decade. However, Facebook saw an opportunity to use this information—people's personal details, behaviors, and habits—and exploit those who trusted it to handle that information ethically. It began to package and sell this data so that companies could target markets and, as we now know, even influence peoples' thinking about social and political issues. People were co-opted (brainwashed) by sinister campaigns that would post fabricated stories and information to sway their thinking or to incite consternation.

Sadly, this also happened because of greed. The values set at Facebook were focused on growth and expansion, not on being custodians of peoples' personal information.

Both cases illustrate a failure in managing company culture. In the past, these companies presumably had noble, admirable, and ethical intentions, but those things were not translated over time into the culture by leadership, which failed to (1) set the vision, (2) have a strategic plan, and (3) get people excited and get them on board.

When things went off the rails, it did enormous damage to each company. When values are made clear, public, and are talked about and validated, it is our experience that the people align with those values and behave consistently with them. When they are not clear, people are left to do whatever else they might do because there's nothing guiding the course and, therefore, behavior. The key is to have leadership set the values of the company, make those values clear and public (i.e., displayed visibly), roll them out to the employees, and keep revisiting and reinforcing them in order to validate them. When this happens, companies stay the course; they live and breathe those values. In short, culture drives behavior.

CHARITABLE ORGANIZATIONS

As promised in an earlier chapter, here is a list of charitable organizations that I have found to be legitimate, valuable, and difference making—in other words, the money that you donate actually goes towards making a visible difference. I have given to almost all of the following organizations:

ASPCA
Shriners Hospitals for Children
4ocean
March of Dimes
American Red Cross
Make a Wish Foundation
Doctors Without Borders
St. Jude's
Sierra Club Foundation
UNICEF
American Heart Association
Girl Scouts of America
Save the Children
United Way
Mayo Foundation for Medical Education and Research
American Cancer Society
National Geographic Society
Museum of Modern Art
Public Broadcasting Service (PBS)
Smithsonian Institution

However, it's best for you to research what most aligns with your purpose in giving.